ok is to be returned on or before

Abbeys, Priories and Cathedrals

Abbeys, Priories
and
Cathedrals

A Balfour Book, printed and published by Photo Precision Ltd.
St. Ives, Huntingdon, England.

FIRST EDITION 1973

726
ABB

PRINTED AND PUBLISHED IN GREAT BRITAIN BY
BALFOUR PUBLICATIONS (PHOTO PRECISION LTD.)
ST. IVES, HUNTINGDON, ENGLAND.

ISBN 0 85944 004 4

Contents

SECTION ONE — ABBEYS AND PRIORIES

An outline of British Monasticism   9

I—BENEDICTINE HOUSES
Glastonbury Abbey, Somerset   13
Lindisfarne Priory, Holy Island, Northumberland   14
Whitby Abbey, Yorkshire   15
Bath Abbey, Somerset   16
Buckfast Abbey, Buckfastleigh, Devonshire   16
Dunfermline Abbey, Fifeshire   18
Wymondham Abbey, Norfolk   19
Sherborne Abbey, Dorset   20
Romsey Abbey, Hampshire   21
Pluscarden Priory, Morayshire   22
Prinknash Abbey, Gloucestershire   23

II—AUGUSTINIAN HOUSES
St. Osyth Abbey, Essex   25
Waltham Abbey, Essex   25
Christchurch Priory, Hampshire   27
Worksop Priory, Nottinghamshire   28
Bolton Priory, Yorkshire   28
Inchcolm Abbey, Fifeshire   29
Jedburgh Abbey, Roxburghshire   30
Cartmel Priory, Lancashire   31

III—CISTERCIAN HOUSES
Furness Abbey, Lancashire   33
Neath Abbey, Glamorgan   34
Tintern Abbey, Monmouthshire   34
Rievaulx Abbey, Yorkshire   36
Fountains Abbey, Yorkshire   37
Melrose Abbey, Roxburghshire   38
Dundrennan Abbey, Kirkcudbrightshire   39
Kirkstall Abbey, Yorkshire   40
Sweetheart Abbey, Kirkcudbrightshire   42

IV—OTHER HOUSES
Castle Acre Priory, Norfolk   43
Dryburgh Abbey, Berwickshire   44
Egglestone Abbey, County Durham   44
Caldey Abbey, Caldey Island, Pembrokeshire   45

SECTION TWO — CATHEDRALS

Cathedrals of Britain   47

I—BUILT FOR BENEDICTINE MONKS
Gloucester Cathedral, Gloucestershire   49
Worcester Cathedral, Worcestershire   50
Canterbury Cathedral, Kent   51
St. Albans Abbey, Hertfordshire   53
Rochester Cathedral, Kent   54
Ely Cathedral, Cambridgeshire   55
Durham Cathedral, County Durham   57
Norwich Cathedral, Norfolk   58
Peterborough Cathedral, Huntingdonshire   58

II—BUILT FOR OTHER MONASTIC ORDERS
Dunkeld Cathedral, Perthshire   61
Southwark Cathedral, London   63
Glasgow Cathedral, Lanarkshire   64
Bristol Cathedral, Gloucestershire   66
Brechin Cathedral, Angus   67

III—BUILT FOR SECULAR CANONS
York Minster, Yorkshire   69
Lincoln Cathedral, Lincolnshire   70
Hereford Cathedral, Herefordshire   72
Chichester Cathedral, Sussex   73
Ripon Cathedral, Yorkshire   75
Exeter Cathedral, Devonshire   76
Kirkwall Cathedral, Mainland, Orkney Islands   77
Dornoch Cathedral, Sutherland   78
Wells Cathedral, Somerset   79
Lichfield Cathedral, Staffordshire   80
St. David's Cathedral, Pembrokeshire   81
Salisbury Cathedral, Wiltshire   82
St. Asaph Cathedral, Flintshire   84
St. Machar's Cathedral, Aberdeen   85
Beverley Minster, Yorkshire   85

IV—POST MEDIEVAL CATHEDRALS
St. Paul's Cathedral, London   87
Birmingham (Anglican) Cathedral, Warwickshire   88
Westminster Cathedral, London   90
Liverpool (Anglican) Cathedral, Lancashire   91
Guildford Cathedral, Surrey   91
Coventry Cathedral, Warwickshire   92

Glossary   93

Index to Illustrations   96

Foreword

Our abbeys and priories, surviving either in ruined form or as regularly attended one-time abbey churches, are among the architectural and historic glories of Great Britain. Their variety is considerable, and because many of them were first established in remote places they now frequently stand in picturesque surroundings. In the first section of this book some 32 monastic houses have been chosen for illustration, ranging from ruins that provide little more than a hint of how they must once have looked to thriving modern monastic communities.

To this is added a second section illustrating and describing 35 cathedral churches in England, Wales and Scotland, almost all of them in regular use. Many of these were in fact first built as abbey churches, becoming cathedrals only after the dissolution of the monasteries under Henry VIII.

In the first section the illustrations are arranged so that religious houses belonging to the same order fall within the same sub-division. The houses are described chronologically within these sub-divisions. In the second section the cathedrals are similarly divided into categories, and then arranged chronologically within them. At the back of the book will be found an explanatory glossary of ecclesiastical terminology, which, in addition to providing definitions of technical terms, explains numerous historical and sectarian aspects of both monasticism and the Church in general.

Section One — Abbeys and Priories

AN OUTLINE OF BRITISH MONASTICISM

Monasticism first came to England in AD 597 at the instigation of St. Augustine when he reintroduced Christianity to these shores. Initially the movement was of a purely missionary character and was confined to the southern part of England, though it rapidly spread to other parts. The initial impact of the Augustinian rule was not however destined to flourish to any marked extent for it was overshadowed by that of the Benedictines, introduced into Britain during the second half of the seventh century by Bishop Wilfrid of Ripon.

This was the first of the truly powerful orders to hold sway in British monastic circles, though the magnificent surviving ruins of some of the great Benedictine foundations do not date from this first era of Benedictine might. Indeed, initially Benedictinism endured for only about two centuries, Danish and other invaders inflicting marked damage on monastic properties to the extent that by the middle of the tenth century monasticism had virtually ceased to exist in this country and those houses that survived, usually the smaller properties, became nothing more than the private domains of landed families wishing to avoid excessive taxation by assuming the guise of sanctity.

A rebirth occurred almost immediately, again under the sway of the Benedictine rule, this time at Glastonbury under St. Dunstan. At the same time other abbeys were founded at Abingdon and Ely; then, under the auspices of King Edgar (959-

975), a meeting was held of the heads of all religious houses, resulting in about the year 970 in the drafting of a code of observance known as the 'Regularis Concordia'.

It was during Edgar's brief reign that the second significant era of British monasticism was initiated, one in which the religious foundations came to play a marked role in the government of the country, and more important, they became virtually the only harbingers of learning and artistic activity in the land.

By 1066 there were 35 monasteries and nine large nunneries in England, all of them observing the Benedictine rule; they were situated almost exclusively in the southern portion of England. With the coming of the Normans, and William's determination to control the religious life of the nation, a complete change was instituted, led by the appointment of Norman heads of all the religious foundations.

From posterity's point of view this change produced great advantages, leading to the erection of many fine new ecclesiastical buildings. About the year 1100 a number of new abbeys were established, including William's own abbey of Battle and those at Chester and Selby. A further notable trend at this time was a spreading northwards, the great foundations of the north of England and Scotland stemming directly from the work of a band of three monks from Evesham, led by one Aldwin, who over a period of only twenty years increased their number to 100 and established such important abbeys as that at Whitby, as well as many lesser establishments. When it is considered that the usual complement for the establishment of a new religious house was an abbot and twelve monks this achievement appears even more remarkable.

It was a time of great monastic activity. During this same period the Cluniac monks—taking their name from the parent abbey at Cluny in Burgundy—were establishing themselves in southern England, the abbey at Lewes being founded in 1077. By the year 1135 there were some 11 Cluniac monasteries in England. In that the Cluniacs observed the parentage and token authority of the Burgundian abbey from which they took their name they were quite different from any other English monastic order.

Next however to the Benedictines it was the Cistercians who exerted the most marked influence on English monastic life, taking their name from the abbey at Cîteaux and observing the Benedictine rule. They first became established in England in the year 1128, when the abbey at Waverley, Surrey, was founded. In 1132 they established the great abbey at Rievaulx in Yorkshire, bestowing upon the order its first true significance in this country and opening the way for a total of 40 Cistercian foundations in England by the year 1152, with several others in Scotland and Ireland.

During the thirteenth century there was an influx of Dominican and Franciscan preaching friars. These men differed from the monks of the Cistercian and Benedictine orders in that they became established in the principal towns and cities throughout the country, eschewing remoteness. They were followed by many lesser orders of friars, including the Hermits of St. Augus-

tine, the first of whom reached England c.1242, establishing some 35 religious houses over the ensuing century.

These were not the only followers of the Augustinian rule in England, although until about the year 1100 Augustinian monasteries had tended to be smaller than other houses, usually being attached to cathedrals and other churches. A more ambitious form of Augustinianism came about during the reign of Henry I, flourishing during the reign of Stephen, its houses in the main differing from the older Augustinian houses in that they were established as independent entities, not, as previously, being necessarily attached to a church. Most of these new Augustinian houses were accorded priory rank—that is, junior to an abbey but not, as with the other orders, subordinate to an abbey.

Augustinianism continued to prosper in Britain, with new foundations appearing right up to the latter part of the thirteenth century. Like other houses, they fell into a condition of decline in the mid fourteenth century. Part of the cause was the Black Death, beginning 1348-49, which led to a lowering of numbers in religious houses. A further cause was the worsening of relations between Great Britain and France, where most of the religious orders had their parent houses. After the year 1350, until the time of the dissolution almost two centuries later, the total number of new houses of all kinds was a mere 20 or less.

Few monastic establishments actually closed so that by the reign of Henry VIII there were altogether some 900 monasteries scattered throughout the country. 48 houses belonging to the Knights Templars had been suppressed over the period 1308-12; about 70 alien priories were suppressed between 1350 and 1414 and a small number of houses were closed during the last decades of the fifteenth century at the instigation of Cardinal Wolsey. It was Henry VIII, however, who directed the final closure of all monastic houses in England and Wales. This he achieved by Act of Parliament and attainder over the years 1536-40, confiscating all properties connected with the monasteries. Only about six communities went into exile to continue their monastic lives; and today only Syon Abbey in Devon survives. All other monastic foundations in Britain date from much later times.

Ostensibly Henry's purpose in suppressing the monasteries was to counter what he termed their corruption; in fact his purpose was to replenish his own coffers from the proceeds of their spoliation. In one gesture Henry effectively terminated the growth in learning and creativity that the abbeys and priories had fostered; he spared no thought for the dreadful destruction that would inevitably follow of some of the finest existing examples of medieval architecture, nor did he trouble to preserve precious manuscripts and other artefacts. Today only the ruins of these magnificent old structures remain, though fortunately many of the churches that were at one time attached to monasteries have enjoyed a greater measure of good fortune and are still in regular use for worship, their surrounding domestic buildings having long before disappeared.

Scottish monasticism developed in the wake of English and Welsh monasticism. At the time of the dissolution King James V of Scotland refused to follow Henry VIII's policy, however much the English monarch tried to persuade him to do so. Instead he obtained from the Pope a bull enabling him to tax the Church (in principle incorporating the guarantee that the monasteries would continue to exist in a Scotland that was still obedient to the Church of Rome). The result, naturally, was that the monasteries fell behind hand in paying their dues. In order to rescue their foundations from debt abbots were one by one led to resort to the Scottish recourse of 'heuing', or granting hereditary tenure of the lands to other parties. Inevitably this led to monasteries being closed down and their lands being transferred to temporal lordships confirmed by Acts of Parliament.

Glastonbury Abbey

I BENEDICTINE HOUSES

GLASTONBURY ABBEY
Somerset

Legend has attached many traditions to this foundation, the cradle of English monasticism. It is said that the first church here was actually established by some of Christ's first disciples, and that there was a Christian settlement of some kind on the site as early as the second century. Of even more pronounced legendary character is the association of Glastonbury with St. Joseph of Arimathea and the so-called Holy Grail, traditionally a receptacle containing some of both the blood and sweat of Jesus Christ, later incorporated into the Arthurian cycle and leading to the belief that both King Arthur and his Queen, Guinevere, were buried here.

Whether any of these assertions can be substantiated is doubtful; even so the foundation at Glastonbury is very old, and can be dated with reasonable confidence to the sixth century, a charter being possibly granted as early as the year 601. It was refounded by Ine, King of Wessex, c.705. It was here, in the year 940, that St. Dunstan, the abbot, introduced the Benedictine rule into Britain, thereby setting into motion the great stream of monastic activity that soon after began to flow.

The abbey immediately prospered, though fire destroyed many of the buildings in 1184, and by 1199 there were some 49 monks in the house. Tragedy came to Glastonbury at the time of the dissolution, for the abbot, Richard Whyting, refused voluntarily to surrender his monastery to

Glastonbury Abbey—
The Abbot's Kitchen

the King's men, and for his disobedience, together with two of his monks, he was hanged on nearby Glastonbury Tor, the usual penalty for those who refused to meet the monarch's will.

LINDISFARNE PRIORY
Northumberland

Lindisfarne, on Holy Island just off the Northumberland coast, is lastingly associated with the name of St. Cuthbert, though the remains of the monastery that may be inspected today stem from a much later date than the era of his residence here. The original abbey, as it then was, was established in the year 635 by Oswald, King of Northumbria, for St. Aidan, a Celtic monk from Iona. This foundation prospered, until in 875 it suffered under the Danish invaders and the monks fled, bearing the remains of St. Cuthbert which they eventually deposited at Durham, the abbey falling beneath the merciless hands of the invaders.

The present priory ruins date from 1083, a new church being erected in 1093; the foundation itself was dependent upon Durham. Lindisfarne was never heavily populated, the number of monks varying between five and nine. The abbey was built from red sandstone, and even today sufficient remains in ruined state for the visitor to comprehend something of the priory's original appearance, situated on an island that later became a minor military stronghold, causing the monastic buildings themselves to be fortified.

Lindisfarne Priory

14

Whitby Abbey

WHITBY ABBEY
Yorkshire

The history of Whitby is intimately associated with that of Lindisfarne, for those same Danes who sacked the island abbey also razed Whitby. Like Lindisfarne, the buildings that stand in ruins at Whitby today stem from a much later date than the abbey's first foundation, which took place about the year 675, when King Oswy granted the property to St. Hilda to found an abbey dedicated to St. Peter for both men and women.

Following the Danish destruction of 867 Whitby's ruins lay dormant until after the Norman conquest; then William granted the property to one of his followers, one Reinfrid, who gave the house the name of the monastery of St. Peter and St. Hilda. Whitby at first enjoyed only priory status, becoming a full abbey at some time before the year 1109, and a mitred abbey by the fourteenth century.

The last abbot of Whitby was Abbot de Vall, who in 1539 surrendered the abbey to Henry VIII's men—or 'visitors' as they were called—without demur, knowing full well that opposition, as had been the case elsewhere, would only lead to hanging, drawing and quartering. Because he made no protest the building did not suffer too drastically at the outset, being stripped simply of its valuables. Time and the elements however took over where King Henry's men had been reasonably lenient, and the abbey soon fell into a state of ruin. Happily an impressive portion of the structure remains and, set against its stark background, it still presents the visitor with an impressive aspect.

BATH ABBEY
Somerset

Bath is so inseparably associated first of all with the Romans and later with the gracious eighteenth century and the age of Beau Nash that it is hard to call to mind the ancient ecclesiastical heritage of this lovely city. Yet the fine abbey church, in itself not a particularly ancient structure, stands as a firm reminder of an era when Bath was an important ecclesiastical centre.

A house of nuns is recorded as having been established here as long ago as the late seventh century, while there are records of a community of monks dedicated to St. Peter dating from 758, the monastery possibly being rebuilt in the year 775. Apart from the church all the monastic buildings disappeared at the time of the suppression, the property being surrendered to the King's men in January, 1539.

Today the abbey church, standing alongside the old Roman baths, restored in 1603 to repair much of the damage that the original 1499 church had suffered under the dissolution, is an impressive monument to a monastic past that all but vanished from Great Britain under the rapacious direction of a tyrant monarch.

BUCKFAST ABBEY
Devonshire

The original abbey at Buckfast was of the Benedictine order, apparently being first founded in the year 1018 by King Canute, at the instigation of one Aylward. Following the Norman conquest the abbey prospered but in the year 1136 it became Savignac in its avocation, later transferring to the Cistercian rule.

Situated on the fringe of Dartmoor, Buckfast Abbey's history was for a long time obscure, until the chance discovery of a piece of a parchment book transpired to be a part of the abbey's cartulary, recording the names of certain of the abbots, those of early benefactors of the abbey and other items of information. One early benefactor was the Baron of nearby Totnes Castle; he it was who gave lands to the monks from Normandy following the conquest, charging them with singing a daily mass for the welfare of the souls of himself and his wife.

Other fragments of information have survived but by and large little is known of the life led at Buckfast which was more than likely one that followed strictly the severe Cistercian rule. In the year 1349 there was a great plague in Devon, and it is almost certain that the monks here would have suffered a depletion of numbers because of it. The last abbot was Gabriel Dunne, probably appointed specifically because he would offer no opposition to the King's men when they suppressed the monastery in 1539, Dunne receiving an annuity of £120 for his co-operation and his nine monks all being granted pensions.

The great abbey church at Buckfast has only survived in rebuilt form, the site having been reoccupied by Benedictine monks in 1882. It was not however until the year 1907 that the newly established community was enabled to begin rebuilding, a task that was completed in 1938, standing today as a firm reminder of Buckfast's long history.

Buckfast Abbey

DUNFERMLINE ABBEY
Fifeshire

One of the largest of the Scottish monasteries, Dunfermline was founded by Queen Margaret about the year 1070. It was originally only of priory rank, dependent upon Canterbury and instituted by monks sent from there by Archbishop Lanfranc, but it became a full abbey under the auspices of King David of Scotland in 1128. Geoffrey, prior of Canterbury, became the first abbot of Dunfermline.

The abbey church, which is the only part of the abbey that survives in an unruined condition, was dedicated in 1150, and in 1245 Pope Innocent IV allowed the abbot the dignity of a mitre. In 1303 King Edward I was responsible for the destruction of many of the abbey's domestic buildings, with further destruction taking place during 1560 by the reforming lords. In 1589 the Lordship of Dunfermline was granted to Queen Anne, wife of King James VI of Scotland, later James I of England.

Dunfermline's founder, Margaret, was the daughter of the Saxon Edward Aetheling. She married King Malcom III of Scotland in 1068 and founded Dunfermline, the first of the medieval religious houses in Scotland, immediately following her move to Scotland. The abbey is impressive both for its historical significance and for its large size. Today, viewing the ruined walls of the one-time monastery, it is still possible to conceive it as it was during the days of its eminence.

Dunfermline Abbey

Wymondham Abbey

WYMONDHAM ABBEY
Norfolk

The abbey church of St. Mary and St. Thomas of Canterbury at Wymondham is at once recognisable by its two quite different towers, one of them built after the customary square fashion and the other octagonal in shape. Very little of the one-time establishment apart from this abbey church, itself a partial ruin, has survived. The story of the foundation is, however, of interest.

It was founded as a priory dedicated to St. Mary by William de Albini in the year 1107, originally as a dependency of St. Albans Abbey. It became a full abbey at the request of the prior in 1449. At this time there would probably have been some 14 monks in residence, though the original priory had been endowed to contain 20. At the time of the dissolution there were only ten monks.

Today the abbey church is still in use, the principal ornament of the town of Wymondham. The old choir has completely disappeared, but the nave remains, graced by a fine hammer-beam roof. It is interesting to note that the two towers came into existence at different times, and for different reasons: the original octagonal tower dates from about 1400, while the square west tower was erected half a century later by the parish, the disparity arising from protracted disagreement over what kind of tower should be built.

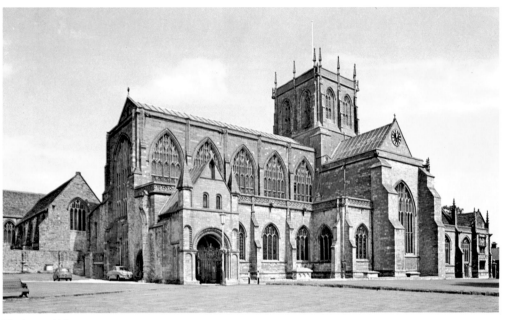

Sherborne Abbey

SHERBORNE ABBEY
Dorset

The abbey church at Sherborne was founded in the year 705 as the seat of a bishop with authority over the west Saxon see of Dorchester, including the whole of the counties of Berkshire, Wiltshire, Somerset, Dorset, Devon and Cornwall. Distinction came to the establishment immediately following its foundation, for the first bishop was St. Aldhelm, who is said to have been the first Englishman ever to have written in Latin and, on his own account, the introducer of poetry into this country. Sherborne ceased to be an episcopal seat in 1078 following its merging twenty years earlier with Ramsbury to form the new diocese of Salisbury.

It was Bishop Wulfsige, in 993, who first introduced Benedictine monks to Sherborne and King Aethelred granted

the abbey a charter in 998. Sherborne was not finally created an abbey until 1122, when some 50 monks were in residence. This number was drastically reduced over the course of the ensuing two centuries so that by the time of the dissolution there were a mere 16 monks, including among their number two dependent priors.

Following the changeover to abbey status much rebuilding and alteration took place at Sherborne, most of the present abbey church dating from the fifteenth century, although certain older architectural features are still in evidence. Accidental fire alas attacked the church in 1436, arising from a dispute between the townsfolk and the abbot regarding the parish's right to use the abbey church for public worship, and all that survived of the original edifice was the Lady Chapel and the porch. It required until almost the end of the fifteenth century to complete the rebuilding, the last work carried out by the monks, who handed the abbey over to the King's men in 1539.

Sherborne today contains many treasures, but perhaps the most unusual is the lovely glass reredos engraved by Laurence Whistler in 1968.

ROMSEY ABBEY
Hampshire

The abbey of St. Mary and St. Elfreda at Romsey, a nunnery, was probably founded about the year 907. Its founder was King Edward the elder, his daughter Elfreda becoming the first abbess. It became a Benedictine house, under the auspices of the gentle King Edgar, in 967. The Danish invaders rendered it little more than a ruin in the closing years of the tenth century but it was quickly rebuilt.

All that remains today is the magnificent abbey church, a mainly Norman relic that also embodies elements of the Early English architectural style. At the time of the dissolution Romsey contained some 25 nuns who at first resisted the King's demands to make over their property to his men. They were unsuccessful in their opposition and in 1539 they had at last to abandon their home, the domestic buildings attached to the foundation being accordingly demolished. The church survived, not on account of any care for its fabric by the King's men but rather by the munificence of the townsfolk, who in 1545 raised £100 towards the preservation of the structure.

Romsey stands today as the foremost relic of a nuns' church in Great Britain. Its history, apart from destruction and eventual dissolution, is by and large uneventful—with the singular exception of the story of King Stephen's daughter Mary, who during the early twelfth century was removed from the nunnery to marry Mathew of Flanders, becoming Countess of Boulogne

Romsey Abbey

but eventually having to return to Romsey and finally becoming the abbess there. As a building, Romsey possesses many fine features, particularly its superb nave with seven bays, the majority of them Norman in origin. Among the more unusual features of the abbey, and a fourteenth century innovation, are two east windows.

PLUSCARDEN PRIORY
Morayshire

Dependent upon Dunfermline Abbey, Pluscarden Priory was founded by King Alexander II in 1230, his charter being granted in 1236. Originally the house followed the order of Vallis Caulium, said to have been introduced into Scotland in 1230 and wholly dependent upon a mother house of Val de Choux in Langres in France. Pluscarden was one of only three such houses in Scotland, sometimes referred to as Cistercian but actually becoming Benedictine in 1454.

It was in 1453 that Pope Nicholas V, at the instigation of the Benedictine prior of Urquhart, where there were only two monks as against six at Pluscarden, agreed that Pluscarden should be separated from its mother house and placed under the authority of Dunfermline. Its history thereafter was without marked incident, and in 1587, by act of the Scottish Parliament, it was created the property of the free barony of Alexander Seton.

The story of Pluscarden does not however close with this occurrence; for following abandonment and subsequent ruination, after a lapse of some three centuries

Pluscarden Priory

Prinknash Abbey

it came once again into the hands of ecclesiastical authorities. It was offered first of all in 1920 by Lord Calum Crichton-Stuart to the Benedictine monks established on Caldey Island in South Wales. They were unable to afford the property at that time, but finally the monks of Prinknash Abbey, described next in these pages, felt able to undertake the upkeep of the priory, then virtually no more than a ruin. This took place in 1948, and even today, after several years of occupation, the monks are obliged to lead a hardy existence, contending with many privations arising from the foundation's condition of disrepair. That it should have been reoccupied at all is a matter for congratulation, placing it among the more unusual of medieval monastic remains in Great Britain.

PRINKNASH ABBEY
Gloucestershire

The modern abbey at Prinknash stands as a monument to monastic enterprise and industry during the twentieth century and it is also a considerable architectural achievement. The original foundation dates back several centuries, at least to the year 1526 when the old property was expanded to provide a manor for the Benedictine abbots of Gloucester. The last abbot of Gloucester died within months of the dissolution, the monks surrendering the abbey to the Crown in 1540 and the manor of Prinknash thereafter passing into the hands of numerous different private individuals.

Sir John Bridgeman purchased the property during the early seventeenth century

Prinknash Abbey—
From The West

and set about restoring the lovely medieval chapel attached to the house, still intact and one of the principal attractions to this day. This did not however denote imminent transformation back into a monastic institution, and it was not until 1928 that Benedictines from Caldey Island moved to Prinknash and restored the property to its original dignity, following the invitation made by its owner, Thomas Dyer Edwardes, in 1924.

At first the old manor house was utilised as the monastery, the old abbey at Caldey being sold to a Cistercian community. It was in 1939, after the number of novices had increased appreciably, that an entirely new monastery was first proposed, although the Second World War interfered with positive developments. Following the war, in 1947, the plans forged ahead, monks working in collaboration with the architect to erect what is undoubtedly one of the most impressive modern monastic structures in Europe, consecrated as recently as 1972.

Benedictinism embodies the belief that residential religious foundations should be self-supporting. Because of this the monks at Prinknash have formed themselves into a well organised semi-industrial community, manufacturing among other things the world famous Prinknash pottery (wrought from locally obtained clay) and incense.

II AUGUSTINIAN HOUSES

ST. OSYTH ABBEY
Essex

The flint and stone gateway of St. Osyth Abbey is one of the most graceful examples of monastic architecture in Britain. Usually referred to as St. Osyth Priory, the foundation became a full abbey at some date prior to 1161, having been established as an Augustinian priory earlier in the century. It is built on the site of a much earlier monastic foundation, a nunnery dedicated to St. Osyth who was slain by the Danes in 653 or possibly later.

The present abbey was founded by Richard de Belmeis, Bishop of London, for canons of Holy Trinity, London, who moved to St. Osyth in 1121. The priory was dedicated to Saints Peter and Paul, as well as to St. Osyth. Originally there were some 30 canons, but by the end of the fourteenth century there were only ten of them. The abbey was surrendered in July, 1539, and the canons and abbot were all granted a pension.

WALTHAM ABBEY
Essex

Waltham Abbey is known also under the name of 'Holy Cross', an allusion to the supposedly miraculous properties of a cross brought to Waltham during the reign of King Canute. The story of its origination is of interest, for a smith was said to have dreamt that if he travelled to

St. Osyth Abbey—
The Gateway

Waltham Abbey

Waltham Abbey—The Gateway

Montacute in Somerset he would find a crucifix buried on a hill there. He made the journey and, together with a procession of local people headed by the parish priest and after a good deal of excavation, they found a black marble crucifix. In order to ascertain where the cross should finally be laid to rest it was placed on a carriage drawn by twelve red oxen and twelve white cows, the spot at which the beasts stopped, guided by providence, being adopted. It was of course at Waltham that they stopped.

The Lord of Montacute then established two priests to be the guardians of the cross at Waltham. This therefore was the origin of Waltham Abbey, transformed by King Harold into a collegiate church with a dean and twelve secular priests. The new church was dedicated in 1060. In 1177 it was transformed once again, this time into a priory for 16 Augustinian canons; it became an abbey in 1184, being mitred at a later date. Waltham was a comparatively large establishment with a complement of 30 or more canons and several lay brothers. It suffered during the time of the Black Death, its numbers being much reduced. It can claim the distinction of being the last British abbey to surrender to Henry VIII under the dissolution. All that remains today is the abbey church and a ruined gatehouse.

CHRISTCHURCH PRIORY
Hampshire

The priory at Christchurch existed first of all as a collegiate church, containing some 24 canons, established probably during the early decades of the eleventh century but conceivably a good deal earlier. Originally there was one main church sur-

rounded by a cluster of nine smaller churches. These were pulled down by Flambard, later to become Bishop of Durham, to enable the building of the large new church that stands to this day, a magnificent example of Norman ecclesiastical architecture. The tower was added during the fifteenth century.

It was in 1150 that Hilary, Bishop of Chichester, succeeded in persuading the establishment's patron, Richard de Redver, son of the Earl of Devon, to transform the college into a priory for Augustinian canons, some two dozen in number. Thereafter the priory settled into a peaceful existence, marred in the year 1402 by the rebellion of several of the canons against their prior. Christchurch surrendered to the Crown in November, 1539, the prior and 18 remaining canons all being granted pensions.

Christchurch Priory

WORKSOP PRIORY
Nottinghamshire

Only the twelfth century priory church of St. Cuthbert and St. Mary, together with a well preserved gatehouse lying just to the south of the church, survive to remind one of Worksop's monastic past. The church however is a very fine building, well restored and bearing distinctive twin west towers.

The priory was founded by William de Lovetot at some date soon after 1119, probably taking its first inhabitants from the priory at Huntingdon.

Their numbers remained fairly constant, and even at the time of the suppression there were 16 canons and a prior.

BOLTON PRIORY
Yorkshire

Bolton Priory overlooking the river Wharfe, a picturesque ruin that has survived sufficiently to provide a very firm reminder of how it must once have looked, was founded by William Meschin and his wife Cecilia de Rumilly in 1120 or 1121. It was dedicated to the Blessed Virgin Mary and St. Cuthbert, established first of all at Embsay and moved to Bolton in 1154. Its patroness was Alice de Rumilly and it was originally dependent on the priory at Huntingdon. It was freed from this dependency in 1194.

Being located in the northern half of England, a part of the country heavily fortified with defensive castles, it naturally

Worksop Priory—
The Gatehouse

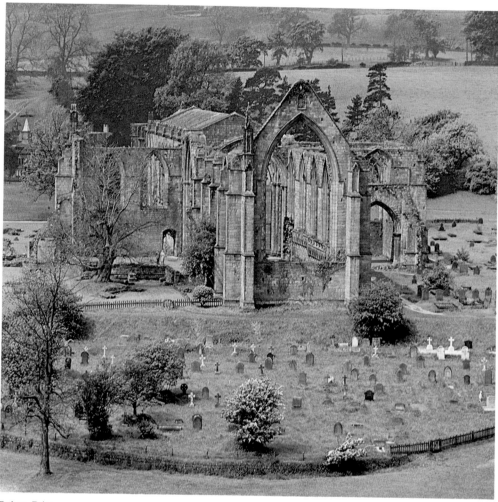

Bolton Priory

stood the risk of damage by Scottish invaders and this occurred in the year 1320, when the monastery suffered to such an extent that many of the canons had to seek temporary refuge in other houses. At this time the personnel of the priory consisted of a prior, 15 canons and two lay brothers. At the time of the suppression there were 14 canons and a prior, who surrendered the house in January, 1540.

INCHCOLM ABBEY
Fifeshire

The Augustinian priory on the island of Inchcolm in the Forth was probably founded about the year 1123, although the earliest charter that has survived dates from 1162-69. The location, however, has more antique ecclesiastical associations than this for it is said that a hermit inhabited the island at a much earlier date. Indeed, it is possible that the surviving medieval church, now a ruin, was built over the site of a full Celtic settlement.

The ruins of the abbey church date from the time of the house's foundation but there is evidence of later additions and alterations right up until the fifteenth century. The house at first fell under the authority of Gregory, Bishop of Dunkeld. The priory was raised to abbey status in 1235. Exactly one century afterwards, in 1335, it is said that the English attacked the property, and again in 1385; and even as late as 1421 the canons were obliged to spend a part of the year on the mainland for fear of English marauders. By 1547 Inchcolm had actually become occupied by the English and about 1564 the community finally removed from the island,

the abbey ceasing to exist even in name by 1578. The abbey and its lands were transferred to temporal lordship for Lord St. Colme in 1609, a charter being granted to him in 1611.

JEDBURGH ABBEY
Roxburghshire

The abbey at Jedburgh was founded first of all as a priory about the year 1138 by King David I of Scotland, the first canons coming from Beauvais. The foundation was elevated to the status of an abbey about 1154. Jedburgh today stands in ruined splendour, a positive reminder of the anomalous sympathies of its medieval

Inchcolm Abbey

canons to the English cause during the troubles of the fourteenth century. But despite the pro-English feelings of an abbot elected in 1296 the abbey suffered desecration when relations between the two kingdoms became fully embittered.

This abbot and his canons were finally obliged to desert their abbey early in 1312, fearing for their lives because of their English sympathies. They fled to Thornton-on-Humber, and twelve years later when they thought it was safe to return to their property they were refused re-admission. Two centuries later, on September 24, 1523, the English burned Jedburgh Abbey, the same thing happening again in 1544 and 1545. In 1606 the property was created a temporal lordship for Alexander, Lord Home.

CARTMEL PRIORY
Lancashire

Cartmel Priory was founded by William Marshall, later Earl of Pembroke, between 1189 and 1194, the original canons coming from Bradenstoke in Wiltshire. The number of canons fluctuated around the number of ten. A dependent cell was established at Kilrush in Ireland about 1201-02 for the purpose of looking after Irish estates owned by the priory.

During the fourteenth century the priory suffered raids by the Scots and numbers became so reduced that there were no more than seven canons in residence. Happily, by the fourth decade of the sixteenth century the numbers had returned to the normal ten, with a total of 38 servants to

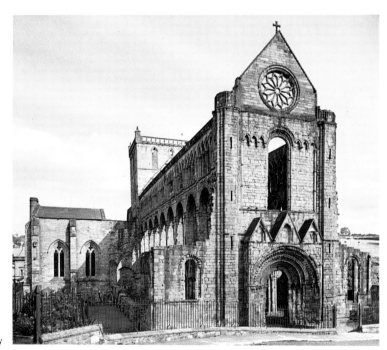

Jedburgh Abbey

Cartmel Priory

look after their needs. The priory was suppressed in 1536, but during the Pilgrimage of Grace it was reoccupied by all the canons with the exception of the prior, who feared the King's forces. The following year, 1537, the priory was suppressed for good, and to emphasise the closure several of the canons, as well as ten local residents unconnected with the religious foundation, were executed.

Today the priory church is preserved in good condition and used for regular worship. Its unusual short tower, set diagonally on top of another, is a particular feature of the church. Among its attractions is a series of fine misericords.

III CISTERCIAN HOUSES

FURNESS ABBEY
Lancashire

The imposing ruins of Furness stand as a memento of the abbey that was established here in the year 1127, one of the largest of Cistercian foundations, though initially it was not of the Cistercian order. The original community of monks had journeyed from Savigny, and had first established their home at Tulketh, founded by Stephen, Count of Boulogne and Mortain and later King of England, in 1124; three years after this it was felt that the site at Furness would be more conducive to monastic life.

From Furness colonies of monks were sent out to establish abbeys in other parts of the country. The abbey became Cistercian only after certain objections by the abbot had been overcome in 1147. The surviving buildings all date from the period immediately following this conversion, their considerable dimensions giving cause for admiration. The dormitory, for instance, was over 200 feet in length.

The complement of monks was always comparatively high in number, and in 1537, at the time of the suppression, there were altogether 39 monks there, many of them connected with the grammar and song schools that were attached to the abbey. Earlier, a number of monks from Furness had accompanied the Pilgrimage of Grace. The monks were forced into surrender in 1537, two of their number having already been imprisoned at Lancaster.

Furness Abbey

Neath Abbey

NEATH ABBEY
Glamorgan

Neath Abbey was the foundation of Sir Richard de Granville and his wife Constance, in the year 1130. Like Furness, it was initially of the Savignac order. The present ruins date however from 1224, the abbey having been burnt down by the Welsh in that year and completely rebuilt to house a complement of 24 monks and 40 or 50 lay brothers. At that time Cistercianism demanded the most austere of existences, but over the ensuing centuries the ways of the monks at Neath, as in other Cistercian houses, became rather more lax, numbers dwindling year by year, so that by the time of the suppression there were but seven monks and an abbot.

In the days of its ascendancy Neath Abbey was one of the finest ecclesiastical structures in Wales, described as possessing a magnificent church. Most of that church has now vanished, the great east window having finally collapsed during the middle of the nineteenth century but it is still possible to discern the outlines of the domestic buildings that were once an integral part of the foundation.

Neath Abbey, in the year 1326, provided a place of refuge for Edward II and the younger Despenser, then fleeing from Bristol. They left Neath Abbey only to be captured soon afterwards.

TINTERN ABBEY
Monmouthshire

Tintern is one of the glories of the Wye Valley; it is also one of the finest surviving Cistercian ruins, an architectural and a monastic monument. Although the neigh-

34

Tintern Abbey

bourhood is fairly heavily populated today, in 1131 when this abbey was founded by Walter FitzRichard, Lord of Lower Gwent and Striguil, the area was remote from civilisation.

This was the reason for it being selected as a site for a Cistercian house and because of this remoteness, following the suppression of the monasteries, Tintern was not resorted to by local farmers and landowners as a general quarry for stone for their own building purposes, and in consequence it has survived in such magnificent condition.

At some time soon after 1220 the abbey was considerably enlarged and the church which is today its principal glory replaced a smaller original church. The foundation was a large one, and probably there were some 20 monks in the abbey, with anything up to 50 lay brothers but by the time of the dissolution there were only 13 monks remaining.

Roger Bigod, Earl of Norfolk, is usually taken to have been responsible for the church, with work on the nave continuing until about 1320. The great east window, 60 feet in height, and the splendid nave, with its six bays, still provide one with a clear impression of how this church must have appeared when first built with its finely traceried windows filled with coloured glass. The choir, or presbytery, is of four bays and the transepts are each of two bays, the north transept still retaining the tracery work in its window.

The last piece of building work to be undertaken at Tintern prior to the dissolution was the construction of a new cloister; this however was never completed. Tintern was finally dissolved in 1539, the property eventually passing into the hands of the

Dukes of Beaufort, who during the nineteenth century took the trouble to preserve the ruined abbey, taking note of its already considerable interest to travellers.

RIEVAULX ABBEY
Yorkshire

Yorkshire became an important location of Cistercian monasteries because the remoteness and the severity of the terrain were such as to appeal to the monks of this order. Among the glories of monastic architecture in the county is the abbey of Rievaulx, standing peacefully on the banks of the river Rie. It was founded in the year 1132, the land having been provided the year previously by Walter Espec. Its first abbot was William, a disciple of St.

Bernard of Clairvaux who had despatched him and his companions to England to found a monastery there.

Rievaulx was immediately fortunate in its benefactors and accordingly the number of monks increased rapidly; to such an extent, indeed, that the abbey was able to despatch monks to other parts of the country to found further Cistercian abbeys. Among these newer foundations was Melrose Abbey in Roxburghshire. An indication of the size of Rievaulx in its heyday may be gleaned from the fact that in 1167 there were said to have been a total of 140 monks together with 500 lay brothers.

Things soon changed markedly. In 1380 there were but 15 monks and three lay brothers. This was however a general tendency in Cistercian houses, which perhaps set themselves too high standards at

Rievaulx Abbey

the outset. Rievaulx produced several remarkable sons, most notable of whom was surely the second abbot, St. Aelred, an historian of considerable prowess, author of the *Genealogia Regum Anglorum,* written to instruct the young prince who later became King Henry II. Aelred suffered throughout his life from poor health, and was seldom free from pain. Rievaulx was dissolved in 1538.

FOUNTAINS ABBEY
Yorkshire

'Our Lady of the Water Springs', or 'Our Lady of the Fountains', such is the correct name of this lovely old Yorkshire ruin. The abbey dates from 1132, originating from the wish of Richard, the sacrist,

and other monks from the Benedictine abbey of St. Mary at York, to live under a stricter rule than was possible there.

Archbishop Thurstan was the immediate benefactor of this establishment, visiting York in 1132 and discovering certain of the monks dissatisfied with their rule. Thirteen of them followed him when he left the abbey, and he it was who eventually settled them at Fountains. The first abbot was Richard, and under his guidance the monks applied to St. Bernard of Clairvaux to be allowed to follow the Cistercian rule. St. Bernard sent one of his own monks to instruct the inhabitants of Fountains, and at the same time some 13 new monks joined the abbey.

These were auspicious beginnings but matters did not follow as smooth a way as could have been desired and before very long the community found itself having to

Fountains Abbey

Melrose Abbey

contend with considerable hardship, leading to the suggestion that the monks should leave Fountains. Fortunately, soon after this Hugh of York resigned his Deanery to retire to Fountains and he inspired a rebirth of fortune. A further setback had to be endured in the year 1147, when the abbey suffered a sacking and razing following a dispute over Archbishop William's deposition. As so frequently happened with monastic establishments, the repairs that followed incorporated a considerable expansion of the property, and by the late twelfth century Fountains could contain upwards of 50 monks and some 200 lay brothers, making it one of the largest abbeys in the country.

Fountains was granted a mitre in the fifteenth century, but a suggestion that it might be transformed into a cathedral failed to come to fruition. It was dissolved in 1539. Today its ruins are extensive, and like other Cistercian houses its remoteness has meant that it has survived more fully than many other abbeys. Almost the entire ground plan of the foundation may be inspected, together with much of the domestic surroundings.

MELROSE ABBEY
Roxburghshire

Melrose has the distinction of being the first Cistercian house established in Scotland, founded in the year 1136 by King David I and taking its first monks from Rievaulx Abbey. Hardly anything remains of the original abbey church apart from a few fragments of the west wall. This is not surprising, since Melrose suffered several times from violence arising from skirmishes with the English from across the border. The impressive church ruins that may be seen today date from various eras throughout the fourteenth, fifteenth and sixteenth centuries, with the barrel-vaulting over the west end of the nave dating from some time after 1618, in which year the building was reoccupied as a Protestant church.

The first abbey church at Melrose was dedicated in 1146, and in the year 1391 the abbot of this large and impressive foundation was granted a mitre. An indication of the abbey's size may be gleaned from the fact that in 1519 there were some 26 monks and abbots contained in Melrose. In 1608 Melrose was made over as a temporal lordship to John Ramsay, Viscount Haddington, created Lord Melrose in 1609. This brought the monastic life of the abbey to an end.

Among Melrose's surviving treasures are a profusion of sculptures and wood carvings, the latter having come about because Melrose was rib-vaulted throughout and numerous opportunities were provided for decorative carving. The stone sculptures include depictions of grotesque figures, saints, musicians and many others.

DUNDRENNAN ABBEY
Kirkcudbrightshire

Like Melrose, Dundrennan Abbey was founded by King David I, but in the year 1142; like Melrose also, it drew its first complement of monks from Rievaulx. As with most Scottish abbeys, Dundrennan suffered desecration at the hands of English troops at various time during the course of its life, leading the abbot in 1299 to demand some £8,000 in compensation from the English monarch, Edward I. In 1328 the monks of Dundrennan again addressed the English King, this time Edward III, for the restoration of certain

Melrose Abbey

Dundrennan Abbey

lands and revenues of which they had been deprived. Dundrennan became a temporal lordship for John Murray, afterwards Earl of Annandale, in 1606, a charter being granted to him in 1609.

The surviving ruins, in a picturesque setting, are most impressive, sufficient remaining of the great abbey church to evoke much of its past grandeur. The west wall and west door are both intact, while the interiors of both transepts provide good examples of the type of architecture favoured by the Cistercians during the twelfth century.

KIRKSTALL ABBEY
Yorkshire

Kirkstall Abbey is the most complete Cistercian ruin in Great Britain, situated on the outskirts of Leeds; so complete is it, indeed, that during the second half of the

nineteenth century there was a move to have the abbey church completely restored, Gilbert Scott being consulted for his opinions about whether it would be possible to undertake such a scheme and returning the answer that it would. The restoration never took place, but even so it is possible to inspect a considerable portion of this old abbey church.

The abbey was founded on a site occupied by a community of hermits headed by Seleth, who had received instruction in a dream that he must leave the south of England to lead a contemplative life in the north. The Cistercians came here in 1152, after the 13 monks and ten lay brothers from Fountains who had established themselves at Barnoldswick in 1147 had decided that the land here was more conducive to cultivation. The abbot was Alexander and the land for his new abbey was granted to him by William of Poictou, at the instigation of the founder of

Kirkstall Abbey

Barnoldswick, Henry de Lacy.

A number of Seleth's hermits decided to join the new establishment, the foundation being laid out to contain some 36 monks and a considerable body of lay brothers.

Numbers dropped significantly during and following the Black Death, but at the time of the suppression there were still 31 monks at Kirkstall. This was one of the last monasteries to surrender to the Crown.

Sweetheart Abbey

SWEETHEART ABBEY
Kirkcudbrightshire

Sweetheart was the last Cistercian monastery to be established in Scotland. It was founded in 1273 by Devorgilla, widow of John Balliol of Barnard Castle, and was colonised by monks from Dundrennan. Like other Scottish houses it suffered at the hands of the English from time to time, and during both 1299 and 1308 the monks applied to the English monarch for financial compensation, totalling some £5,000 or more. In 1397, it is said, the abbey buildings were struck by lightning and suffered severe damage. It was not until the year 1624 that Sweetheart suffered the fate of all Scottish abbeys and was transferred into a temporal lordship, for Sir Robert Spottiswoode.

The ruins to be observed today are quite extensive, with the great west front and east gable of the abbey church both surviving intact. Despite the completeness of the ruin, however, experts opine that a good deal of the detail of the building is of inferior quality. This apart, it is of considerable interest to be able to compare this abbey with that at nearby Dundrennan. Not the least of the attractions of this ruin is its setting, as well as the weathered richness of the sandstone from which it is built.

IV   OTHER HOUSES

CASTLE ACRE PRIORY
Norfolk

Castle Acre Priory was of the Cluniac order, one of the houses established in Britain observing the parentage of the abbey at Cluny. It was dedicated to St. Mary and to Saints Peter and Paul, and founded by William, Earl of Surrey, in 1089. The Earl of Surrey was the son of William de Warenne, the man who had founded the first Cluniac house in this country, the priory at Lewes created in 1077.

Originally the priory, together with its church, was established within the castle walls at Castle Acre; but only a year later the monks moved to the larger site where the present ruins may be inspected. The establishment was a considerable one, founded originally for some 26 monks and increasing to 35 by 1279. At the dissolution in November, 1537 there were but ten monks and a prior.

The Cluniac houses in Great Britain acquired a reputation for extravagance, and during the fourteenth century especially there were certain scandals emanating from this foundation. Today Castle Acre survives as the most impressive Cluniac ruin in the country, and much of its architectural detail can still be appreciated. The hewn stone and flint of which the greater part of the buildings are constructed is particularly attractive, and especially impressive are the prior's lodging and the chapel.

Castle Acre Priory

DRYBURGH ABBEY
Berwickshire

The Premonstratensian abbey at Dryburgh was founded in the year 1150 by Hugh de Murville and received its first complement of monks from Alnwick Abbey in Northumberland. This was the first house of this order to be founded in Scotland, and because of its seniority, in 1390, it was granted possession of the nunnery at Berwick on Tweed. Its history was one of considerable incident, for it suffered at the hands of the English, and was razed to the ground in 1322, in 1385 and again as late as 1523, 1544 and 1545. It was transferred to temporal lordship in 1606, being assigned as the Lordship of Cardross to John, Earl of Mar.

Little has remained, with the exception of some of the church ruins, with a particularly impressive north transept dating from the thirteenth century. There are also quite extensive remains of the old cloisters, as well as a fine chapter house. Its setting beside the Tweed bestows upon Dryburgh a marked beauty and the fact that both Sir Walter Scott and Field Marshal Earl Haig are buried within its confines lends it an additional interest.

EGGLESTONE ABBEY
County Durham

The Abbey of St. Mary and of St. John the Baptist at Egglestone was also of the Premonstratensian order. It was begun about the year 1190, the foundation in all

Dryburgh Abbey

probability of Ralph de Moulton. The first inhabitants came from Easby, numbering at the outset only an abbot and three canons; the numbers quickly increased, but there were probably never more than about 15 canons. From 1272 onwards Egglestone undertook to supply six chaplains for the chapel at Richmond Castle.

Egglestone was assessed as a lesser monastery under the suppression in 1537; accordingly it was refounded, and was not finally dissolved until 1540, in which year the abbot and eight of his canons were awarded pensions. Hardly anything of the abbey at all survives today. It came into the possession of Robert Strelley in 1548, and the buildings were thereafter allowed to deteriorate. A part of its charm today lies in its picturesque setting.

CALDEY ABBEY
Pembrokeshire

Caldey Island is situated just off the Pembrokeshire coast, a location of particular attractiveness for centuries to those of a reclusive disposition. It was known originally as 'Ynys Pyr' after Pyro, an abbot of Celtic times. Monks of one type or another have lived on the island for 1500 years. It was during the twelfth century that the name of Caldey was assumed, and it was in 1131 that the Norman Robert FitzMartin received it as a gift from King Henry I. He gave the island to his mother; she presented it to the Benedictines of Tiron in France. This small community was dissolved by Henry VIII in 1536.

Egglestone Abbey

After several changes of ownership the island came into the possession of the Rev. W. Done Bushell in 1897; he restored the old priory and sold the island to an Anglican Benedictine brotherhood founded in 1896. They built the present monastery between the years 1910 and 1912, were later received into the Roman Catholic Church and then migrated to Prinknash in 1928. They sold the island to members of the Order of Reformed Cistercians, who took possession in 1929. In 1940 there was a serious fire at the monastery, and many buildings, including the church, were destroyed. It was not until 1951 that the church was finally restored.

Today Caldey Island is a busy monastic community, its members living by and large by the work of their own hands, in accordance with the doctrines of Cistercianism. A part of the abbey's income is derived from a brisk tourist trade, as well as from the manufacture of perfume, made by the monks from the gorse and lavender growing on the island and for which Caldey has subsequently become world famous.

Section Two — Cathedrals

CATHEDRALS OF BRITAIN

The medieval cathedrals of Great Britain originated more often than not as monastic churches and most of the buildings illustrated in this section are monastic foundations. Before the time of the dissolution there were only seventeen cathedrals in Britain. At the dissolution certain abbey churches were raised to cathedral status, while even before that time certain abbots had on occasion been allowed the privilege of wearing the mitre.

With the estrangement of the English church from that of Rome all medieval cathedrals became Anglican, so that none of the Roman Catholic cathedrals now in existence in Britain can claim the antiquity of the Anglican buildings with which this publication is most immediately concerned. However, it is important to keep in mind that prior to the time of the dissolution all English cathedrals were subservient to the Church of Rome, as were the monastic houses described in Section I. Continental influences were naturally at play in much of the cathedral construction that took place following the Norman conquest, but the great glory of ecclesiastical architecture in Britain is that it quickly acquired a recognisable and personal identity and such structures as Lincoln are wholly English. Many of the large abbey churches mentioned in the previous section, as at Fountains and Tintern, are now ruined to such an extent that it is only possible to guess at their original glories; in those churches which survived the dissolution in the form of cathedrals it is happily possible to study the architecture and its development in detail.

A cathedral acquires its status by being the seat of a bishop, and although there are many exceptions it is typically a building of considerable dimensions and exuberantly decorated. In the minds of cathedral builders was the desire to create a lovely building dedicated to the glory of God and expressing what they took to be a singular faith and allegiance.

Medieval architecture as it has survived, owing to the tendency for buildings to be pulled down once they have outlived their usefulness, is predominantly church architecture; certainly so in its more flamboyant manifestations. Collective and individual features emerged that are today regarded as being among the wonders of Britain. One may cite for example the glorious octagonal lantern tower of Ely Cathedral, the conception of Alan of Walsingham. Before his time octagonal towers had been unknown in this country, but there were many on the continent.

Common to most cathedrals are the great west entrances, many of them decorated with sculpture and flanked by twin towers. Large richly traceried windows set into the east and west ends of the cathedrals were inseparable from the basic concept of church architecture, and even today many of them still contain fine stained glass. Great central towers and lofty spires, built high for no other reason than to beautify the structures they adorned, each designed uniquely, at once gave cathedrals an immediately recognisable character. Nor should it be forgotten that the great wealth of many of the monasteries made these often extremely sumptuous features possible. It was not religious devotion by itself that allowed the wonders of Wells, Lincoln and Durham cathedrals to come into being.

Just as they were the first of the great castle builders, so the Normans were also the first of the great cathedral builders of Britain. Many of the oldest of our cathedrals and abbey churches are connected directly or indirectly with those clerics who, for their allegiance to William, were granted important bishoprics or abbocies after the Conquest and hardly any Saxon ecclesiastical dignitaries were allowed to retain their positions.

However, despite the grandeur of such buildings as Durham Cathedral, it was with the introduction of the English Gothic architectural style that our cathedrals achieved their greatest magnificence, originating during the thirteenth century and flowering for more than three centuries following. Intricate feats of construction were achieved, graceful flying buttresses began to support tall outside walls broken by numerous windows filled with colourful glass that flooded naves and aisles with a rich play of light. Sculpture flourished, exhibited to marvellous effect for example on the west front of Wells Cathedral, where stone figures set in individual niches cover the entire facade.

It is customary to divide the various periods of English ecclesiastical architecture into distinct epochs, each of which can be shown to have individual characteristics. For the purposes of convenience they may be listed here as, Norman, English Gothic and Renaissance. In the selection which follows certain more recent architectural traits have also been acknowledged.

Norman architecture is in evidence to varying degrees in most of the older cathedrals; indeed, with few exceptions, no features pre-dating Norman times are evident except in certain instances where the crypts of earlier buildings have been preserved. Semi-circular arches, both in doors and windows, together with the massive round pillars that enclose the naves, are the principal features of these churches.

This style of architecture developed towards the close of the thirteenth century into the lovely English Gothic, itself easily divided into three distinct periods: Early English (thirteenth century), Decorated (1250-1370) and Perpendicular (persisting until about 1550). It is with the Gothic style that medieval cathedral architecture in this country is most immediately associated. Arches became narrower and more pointed, basic lines became slowly more vertical, decorative carving became more ornate, particularly in such features as the tracery work of windows and the ornamental bosses to be seen where the vaulting on ceilings converged and intersected.

Renaissance architecture is not so widely represented among English cathedrals, although there are numerous smaller churches in this style. St. Paul's Cathedral in London is however the most perfect example. Like other such English churches, it drew its inspiration from the Italian architecture of a century earlier. Until the advent of the Gothic revival at the close of the eighteenth century, this style, with its gracious neo-classical lines, flourished in Britain.

During the twentieth century there have been many new and exciting developments in church architecture and among them Coventry Cathedral, illustrated in these pages, is undoubtedly one of the most intriguing.

I   BUILT FOR BENEDICTINE MONKS

Gloucester Cathedral, in addition to its integral attractiveness, claims the distinction of having been the setting for William the Conqueror's authorisation of the compiling of the Domesday Book in 1085. The building dates from 1058, in which year Aldred, Bishop of Worcester, began to build a new church for the Benedictine monks established there. As a cathedral, however, Gloucester dates only from the year 1541, one of the earliest of the new sees created by Henry VIII following the dissolution of the monasteries.

The real history of the present structure begins in the year 1072, when Abbot Serlo began a rebuilding programme. His building was finally dedicated in 1100 and graced with a lovely nave, completed in 1089. Thereafter fire played havoc with the church, striking successively in 1102, 1122, 1179 and 1190; on each occasion considerable repair and rebuilding became necessary, rededication taking place in 1239.

Concentrated rebuilding continued, the stone vaulting over the nave, replacing the original Norman wooden vaulting, being built in 1242, and the south west tower being completed in 1246.

Fire struck again in 1300, but the murder of Edward II in 1327 and the placing of his remains in this church, led to thousands of people travelling to Gloucester to worship at his shrine and make gifts to the church, which in turn were used to finance the considerable enrichment of the fabric

Gloucester Cathedral

Worcester Cathedral

that then took place, transforming Gloucester into one of the glories of church architecture in this country.

The work continued throughout the fourteenth and fifteenth centuries, producing such features as the fine Perpendicular choir, completed in 1377, and the addition of a magnificent east window, the largest stained glass window in England, its glass commemorating the knights from Gloucestershire who fought in the Battle of Crecy in 1346. The tower was built in the mid fifteenth century and the Lady Chapel, with its fan vaulting, was completed in 1499.

WORCESTER CATHEDRAL
Worcestershire

The see of Worcester dates back to 680; the present cathedral was begun at some date immediately after 1062, under Bishop Wulfstan, who although he was a Saxon was allowed to retain his bishopric following the Norman conquest. Building continued throughout the twelfth century, and the cathedral was finally dedicated in the presence of Henry III in 1218. A second period of building occurred during the fourteenth century, and much of the nave dates from this time, displaying some fine Decorated work. The great tower was completed under Henry of Wakefield at the very close of the century.

Worcester fared badly at the time of the Civil War, and at various times both Royalists and Cromwellians inflicted damage on the building. It was from the tower of this cathedral, in 1651, that the future King Charles II watched his supporters being routed by Cromwell's troops in the Battle of Worcester. The building was not immediately repaired after the Restoration and it had to wait instead until the eighteenth century; these restorations were in their turn replaced by those of Sir Gilbert Scott during the nineteenth century.

Much of what is today to be seen at Worcester dates from comparatively recent times; there is however a certain amount of Norman work still in evidence, principally in the aisles and transepts. The Early English choir is also of considerable appeal, as is the fine Norman crypt, notable for its profusion of pillars. Among the numerous monuments contained in the cathedral is the tomb of King John, with the earliest effigy of an English king to be found in this country. Prince Arthur's Chantry was built by Henry VII to commemorate his son who had died in 1502.

CANTERBURY CATHEDRAL
Kent

The origins of this pre-eminent church among English cathedrals stem back to the days before St. Augustine's reintro-duction of Christianity to these shores. On the site of the present structure there quite possibly stood a Roman or Romano-British church, and it was this church, together with its palace, that King Ethelbert gave to Augustine after the missionary from Rome had converted the British monarch to Christianity.

The first work of rebuilding at Canterbury following the Norman invasion was undertaken by the first Norman archbishop, Lanfranc, in 1070; this work took seven years to complete, and a Benedictine monastery was erected at the same time, housing some 100 monks. Completed in a hurry, it was not long before it was felt that this church was unworthy of a primate's see; in 1096, therefore, at the time of St. Anselm's primacy, a new building was undertaken. This new church was completed in 1115 and reconsecrated in 1130.

Canterbury Cathedral

St. Albans Abbey

The principal architect of Anselm's church was Prior Ernulf, succeeded by one Conrad who supervised the building of the choir, a feature thereafter always known as 'the glorious choir of Conrad', Alas, this lovely chamber perished in a fire soon afterwards, the Frenchman William of Sens being appointed architect of the new choir, completed in 1184.

It was in Ernulf's original choir, in the year 1170, that St. Thomas à Becket was murdered; his shrine later attracted pilgrims by the thousand.

This grim happening was not however the only violent action to be carried out beneath Canterbury's lofty roof. During the time of the Reformation, in the primacy of Thomas Cranmer, himself destined to burn at the stake, the reformers completely destroyed the shrine of Becket, as well as several other shrines contained within the cathedral. Archbishop Laud repaired the damage, only to see the entire inside of his church reduced to virtual ruin, his windows broken and the fabric destroyed.

The principal restorer of Canterbury was Archbishop Juxon, earlier Bishop of London and attendant of King Charles I on the scaffold at Whitehall in 1649. His work was continued by his successor, Archbishop Sheldon. Restoration and improvement continued over the centuries, including the addition of a fine bishop's throne by Grinling Gibbons. During the nineteenth century Sir Gilbert Scott carried out extensive restoration.

The abbey's principal features include the nave, some 80 feet in height, a particularly impressive east window, a central tower resting on original Norman piers but itself dating from the late fifteenth and early sixteenth centuries, the world's largest Norman crypt, and numerous mon-

St. Albans Abbey—The Gateway

uments commemorating famous men, ranging from the Black Prince's tomb to the monument to the musician and organist, Orlando Gibbons. In addition, there remains a considerable range of the original monastic buildings.

ST. ALBANS ABBEY
Hertfordshire

Pope Adrian IV (Nicholas Breakspear), who had himself been connected with the establishment in the days of his youth, granted the abbey of St. Albans the distinction of being denominated the premier Benedictine monastery in the land. Today, apart from the old gatehouse, nothing remains of the complex of monastic buildings to remind one of the establishment's one-time ecclesiastical grandeur; only the magnificent but much restored cathedral church, with the longest nave to be found anywhere in Great Britain, survives to hint at the lustrous past of this foundation, raised to cathedral status in 1871.

The church is indeed a superb structure, with numerous features of merit; but the history of this one-time abbey is also one of considerable impressiveness. St. Albans dates from the very end of the eighth century, founded by Offa II, King of Mercia, to preserve the shrine of St. Alban and the relics of certain other saintly figures that were said to have been left on the site by St. German of Auxerre when in the year 429 he visited the old church erected by St. Lupus of Troyes in which St. Alban's remains were kept. Offa had these relics transferred to his new abbey.

Originally the monastery contained both men and women, housed in separate quarters, but it is said that the discipline of the establishment left much to be de-

53

sired, and during the reign of the monastic patron King Edgar, in the early 970's, a stricter form of Benedictinism was introduced at St. Albans. During the second half of the eleventh century the nuns were removed elsewhere.

Earlier, in 930, the abbey, like so many others in Britain, had been ransacked by the Danes, and the relics of St. Alban were carried away to Denmark; happily they were later retrieved. Following the Norman conquest, as elsewhere, a Norman abbot was placed in charge of St. Albans and the building of a great abbey church got underway, completed in 1115—though the present structure is predominantly of a later date, the original building having collapsed in the early thirteenth century.

The last abbot at St. Albans was Richard Boreman, formerly prior, to whom fell the task of handing the property over to the King at the dissolution. It is sometimes averred that he was elected to the post primarily because it was felt he would cause no difficulty at the time of surrender.

ROCHESTER CATHEDRAL
Kent

The first Bishop of Rochester, St. Justus, was appointed in the year 604; he was a follower of St. Augustine, who had come to preach in the city soon after his landing in England. Until 1082 the cathedral was looked after by secular canons, but thereafter it became the home of Benedictine monks. It was soon after this date that the monks began the erection of a Norman cathedral. Consecration took place in 1130, in the presence of King Henry I.

Fire struck in both 1138 and 1177, wreaking much damage; further misfortune occurred when King John captured Rochester Castle. However, during the

Rochester Cathedral

54

Ely Cathedral

early decades of the thirteenth century a considerable amount of building took place, and in 1227 the new choir was first used; afterwards a new west transept and a great central tower were begun. By the end of the thirteenth century the new west transept was complete.

During the first half of the fourteenth century a good deal of restoration was undertaken under the auspices of Bishop Haymo, and it was he who completed the central tower. New windows were also added at this time, as was the Lady Chapel, unusually placed on the south side of the nave off the south transept. Today this is the chapel of the King's School.

A large Perpendicular window has been inserted in the west front, but otherwise it presents a fine example of Norman ecclesiastical architecture, with the exception of the northern turret which is a comparatively modern substitution. The nave too is still predominantly Norman, though much

of the rest of the building is in the Early English style.

ELY CATHEDRAL
Cambridgeshire

Ely Cathedral originated from a Saxon nunnery established in this relatively remote part of Great Britain in the year 673, the foundation of Etheldreda, first abbess and patron saint of Ely. As was usual at this time, the house contained both monks and nuns. The present structure was begun in the year 1083 by Abbot Simeon, the monks at Ely having surrendered to the Normans in 1071. Ely was raised to cathedral status early in the twelfth century, following the completion of the east end of the church. The nave and the great west tower both date from the twelfth century, while later parts of the cathedral date from the thirteenth century.

Durham Cathedral

Mishap frequently accompanied the erection and improvement of ecclesiastical buildings, and in 1322, while the Lady Chapel was under construction, the cathedral's great central tower collapsed, destroying a considerable portion of the building as it did so. However, out of the wreckage emerged what is today one of the cathedral's principal glories, the beautiful octagonal lantern tower, the creation of Alan of Walsingham. It was during this same period that the cathedral's Decorated windows were added and the outside walls were raised, the impressive flying buttresses being attached as a result. All of this was the creation of Walsingham, and it is not for nothing that his tomb bears the inscription 'flower of craftsmen'.

Like so many other fine buildings, Ely Cathedral has undergone much damaging 'restoration' over the years, which during the mid nineteenth century included the removal of the Norman stone screen that had stood across the nave for centuries. However, it is the exterior of Ely that is most impressive, its massive west tower and octagon unmistakable from a great distance. Within, the long nave and the fifteenth century hammer-beam roofs of the transepts are equally interesting.

DURHAM CATHEDRAL
County Durham

The present structure of this, one of the most impressive of all English cathedral buildings, dates from 1093, in which year the foundation stone was laid. The story of the foundation however stems back much further in time than this, to the ninth century, when the monks on Lindisfarne Island just off the coast of Northumberland fled under pressure from the Danish invaders. They carried away with them their monastery's most precious relic, the remains of St. Cuthbert, and forthwith set about seeking a new resting place for them. It took them more than a century of wandering, until the year 997, before they finally came to Durham. Here they raised a church of wood, a sanctuary for their saint's bones and the predecessor of the present cathedral overlooking the river Wear.

It required until the fifteenth century for the work of erecting Durham to be completed, but by far the greater part of the work was completed by the year 1133, including the nave, aisles, western towers and entrance, though the upper portions of the western towers were added only in the thirteenth century, and the pinnacles and parapets not until the end of the eighteenth century. The porch also is a late

Durham Cathedral—The High Altar

57

addition, the design of Wyatt and placed in position in 1775.

The view along the nave at Durham is magnificent, the great pillars being some 23 feet in circumference, dating from the time of Bishop Flambard (1099-1128); the stone vaulting of the roof was finished in 1133, this being the first Norman cathedral in England to boast this feature. Another fine Norman feature of Durham is the Galilee Chapel, at one time the Lady Chapel, erected in 1175 by Bishop Pudsey, but considerably altered during the early part of the fifteenth century by Cardinal Langley. There is a fine large window in the north transept; there is also a famous 'rose' window in the east end of the cathedral; but to many, perhaps, one of Durham's most notable possessions is the tomb of the Venerable Bede, the first English ecclesiastical historian, whose original shrine was alas desecrated by Henry VIII's men and exists today as a simple marble slab.

NORWICH CATHEDRAL
Norfolk

This fine cathedral was begun by Herbert Losinga in 1096, work being completed by his successor about the year 1145. Of considerable interest is the fact that Norwich has survived almost as it was built during this Norman period, with its extremely long nave, aisles and fine transepts. Later additions and alterations came about through varying circumstances, including high wind which swept away the original wooden spire in 1361 and lightning which destroyed its successor in 1463. Many of the windows also date from later periods, the result of successive bishops' attempts to secure better lighting

in the cathedral. The principal among these attempts came about directly from the collapse of the spire, when the clerestory of the Norman presbytery was damaged and had to be rebuilt. By the simple process of raising the new presbytery higher than the nave, by some 11 feet, the monks were enabled to insert a succession of windows, many of them with extremely fine tracery work.

It was during the same century that windows were inserted along the aisles, in an endeavour to lighten the lovely nave. The monks accomplished this by raising the aisle walls. The stone vaulting that covers the ceiling of the nave, as elsewhere in this cathedral, was added as a measure to overcome the threat of fire; it was placed in position between 1463 and 1472 by Bishop Walter Lyhart, and certainly adds to the impressiveness of the nave, which to many visitors is Norwich's finest feature.

The spire, a Perpendicular work, was added to the Norman tower towards the end of the fifteenth century; it stands at a lofty 315 feet. Other notable features at Norwich include the great west window, built during the middle of the fifteenth century, the extensive cloisters and some fine stained glass and misericords.

PETERBOROUGH CATHEDRAL
Huntingdonshire

Peterborough's ecclesiastical associations stem back to the year 654. In that year Peada, the son of the King of Mercia, established a monastery there, installing Saxulph as the first abbot. A church was built soon afterwards, but was destroyed by the Danes during the ninth century, being rebuilt in the seventh decade of the

Norwich Cathedral

following century. This church survived until 1116, when fire destroyed it and the present church replaced it, though the foundations of the Saxon church may still be inspected.

The abbot responsible for the fine structure begun in 1117 was John de Sais, but the building was not ready for dedication, by Robert Grosseteste of Lincoln, until 1238, by which date virtually the whole structure as seen today had been accomplished. The minster did not become a cathedral until the time of the dissolution, when Henry VIII created the new see and appointed the last of the mitred abbots as the first bishop.

Peterborough Cathedral—
The West Front

To most people the west front is Peterborough's crowning glory; indeed, this was one of the last parts of the building to be completed before its dedication, being constructed around an already existing Norman front. The old porch was retained (replaced during the fourteenth century), and thus is explained the unusual circumstance of the centre opening being narower than the two side openings that flank it. Even today the frontal vision of Peterborough seems almost perfect; yet originally the rear (or north-western) tower was capped by a wooden spire, and almost certainly a fourth tower and spire was conceived to the south west, which would have completed the overall visual effect. But even without these appendages Peterborough's west front is among the finest in the country.

Much alteration occurred following the first period of concentrated building, but perhaps the most significant alterations took place during the fourteenth and fifteenth centuries, when in the interests of lighting many of the Norman windows were removed to make way for larger frames. It was at the very end of the fifteenth century also that Peterborough was beautified with one of its most lovely features, the fan vaulting of the aisles surrounding the presbytery.

II BUILT FOR OTHER MONASTIC ORDERS

DUNKELD CATHEDRAL
Perthshire

Dunkeld first became a cathedral church in 1107, but it had been established as a monastic church about the year 800, founded by the Pictish King Constantin. The original inhabitants of the monastery were replaced under the first bishop by Augustinian canons. Following the church's promotion to cathedral status a rebuilding programme was initiated, and a new choir was erected between 1220 and 1250; the architecture was Early English in style, but in 1380, at the time of the troubles with the English, the building was razed. Rebuilding began at once, the nave being completed in 1465 by Bishop Lauder.

These were not the only troubled times with which Dunkeld was obliged to contend: poor Lauder himself was once besieged in his own church, the result of his having dared to imprison a member of the clan Robertson, the clansmen attacking the church on Whit Sunday while the bishop was saying mass, and causing Lauder to climb up into the rafters above the choir in order to avoid their arrows. On a later occasion Bishop Gavin Douglas, the translator of Virgil's *Aenid,* was besieged by the Stewarts, who had opposed his appointment to the bishopric. They went so far as to bar the door against

Dunkeld Cathedral

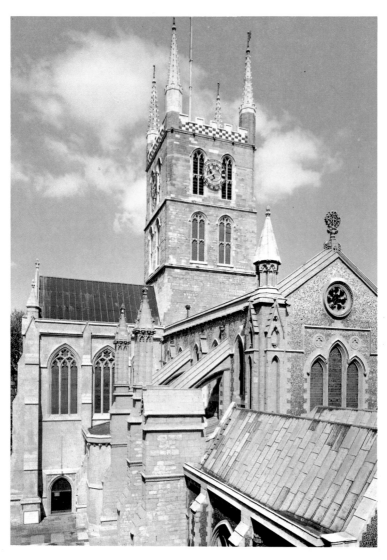

Douglas, and the bishop had to assemble a group of friendly people to assist him in forcing an entry.

Today the nave of this lovely church lacks a roof and over the centuries has become a complete ruin. This came about owing to events immediately following the Battle of Killiecrankie, in 1689, when the cathedral and surrounding properties were occupied by troops, and in the ensuing hostilities suffered severe damage, which has only partially been made good to this day.

The choir however was rebuilt, and this part of the old cathedral is now used as the parish church. The 96 foot tower is still intact, built under Bishop Lauder and completed in 1501. The vault of the Dukes of Atholl is contained in the chapter house, while near its porch is located the grave of Alexander Stewart, Earl of Buchan, frequently nicknamed the 'Wolf of Badenoch'.

SOUTHWARK CATHEDRAL
London

The old church dedicated to St. Marie Overie, subsequently rededicated to St. Saviour, in the historic borough of Southwark just to the south of London Bridge, achieved cathedral status only as recently as 1905. The present building, erected for Augustinian canons, dates from the period immediately subsequent to 1106, though only traces of this have survived, including the wall of the north aisle. Fire struck in 1213, and the opportunity was taken to erect a much larger structure, built under the superintendence of Bishop Rupibus (1205-38).

This rebuilding included both the eastern and western limbs of the church, but only the eastern limb has remained, and that was restored during the nineteenth century. The presbytery and choir are particularly impressive. The nave is en-

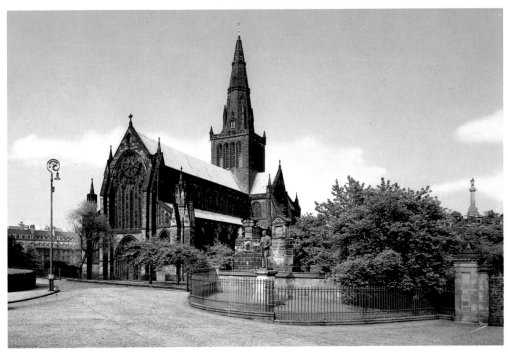
Glasgow Cathedral

tirely modern, dating from the last decade of the nineteenth century though following largely the original Gothic plan.

Southwark Cathedral is of interest today for several reasons; partly because most of the older ecclesiastical buildings north of the river perished during the Great Fire and partly for its numerous historical associations. John Harvard, founder of the famous college in Cambridge, Massachusetts, was baptised here, and there is a Harvard Memorial Chapel to commemorate the fact. Even more intriguing is the fact that William Shakespeare's brother is buried here, and there is both a memorial to Shakespeare and a window dedicated to his memory. Other literary associations can also be claimed for Southwark: the dramatists Massinger and Fletcher are both buried in the cathedral,

as also is John Gower, author of *Confessio Amantis* and friend of Chaucer whose pilgrims in the *Canterbury Tales* began their journey from the nearby Tabard Inn.

GLASGOW CATHEDRAL
Lanarkshire

The Cathedral of St. Mungo in Glasgow was begun in 1124, consecrated in the presence of King James I of Scotland in 1192 and burnt to the ground before 1200. A second cathedral was immediately started, building continuing throughout the thirteenth century. The Early English choir was completed about 1258, and is thought by many to be the finest such

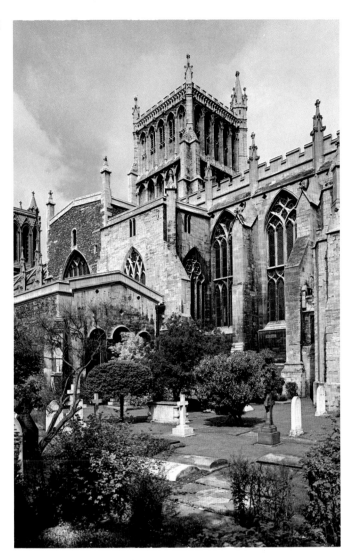
Bristol Cathedral

example in Scotland; it is unusual in that it consists of two distinct storeys, the lower one being the crypt, which is entirely above ground.

The tower and transepts were finished a few years after this. The original wooden steeple suffered the misfortune of being struck by lightning in 1400 and was replaced by a stone one. Thereafter Glasgow Cathedral was fortunate in its circumstances, for throughout the troubled periods with which Scotland had to contend it avoided damage; indeed, it was only during the nineteenth century that any marked alteration occurred in its structure. Then the two western towers were removed and modern glass, almost exclusively by foreign craftsmen, replaced the older glass; the great east window was the gift of Queen Victoria.

This is an attractive cathedral, its sacristy and chapter house dating from the fifteenth century, the latter being built in the Perpendicular style during the time of Bishop Cameron. For a short while, at the close of the fifteenth century, the see of Glasgow became an archbishopric; this ended at the Reformation, when for some time the cathedral lay unused, being restored only when King James VI of Scotland became King James I of England.

BRISTOL CATHEDRAL
Gloucestershire

Bristol has long been a city associated with cultural as well as industrial activities; it is also a city of considerable historic interest, among its particular attractions being the Norman cathedral church founded in the year 1142 by Robert Fitzhardinge, later Lord Berkeley. The original site, tradition has it, covered the spot where the oak stood beneath which St. Augustine first met and offended the British bishops, appearing to them too proud and overbearing. The church, not yet a cathedral, was consecrated in 1148, and extensions to it continued under the

Bristol Cathedral—Norman Chapter House

auspices of Fitzhardinge right up until the year of his death, 1170.

Bristol was one of the new sees created by Henry VIII in 1551; however in 1836 the sees of Bristol and Gloucester were merged, and it was not until 1897 that they were finally separated again. The church was first built to house a community of Augustinian canons, and it was probably Abbot John, at the end of the eleventh or beginning of the twelfth century, who instigated a building programme that led to the structure's substantial extension. He was responsible for the Elder Lady Chapel (Bristol being unusual in possessing two Lady Chapels). However, much of the finest architecture dates back to the first building, including the lovely Decorated chapter house.

The building programme continued through the centuries, including the reconstruction of the choir and choir aisles in the early fourteenth century, under the direction of Abbot Knowle. For his zeal in advancing the church's standing Knowle's successor, Abbot Snow, was awarded a mitre, being granted also a seat in Parliament. Snow also continued the work of extension, adding both the chantry and the Newton Chapel. The Black Death, as elsewhere, interrupted all building plans, and it was not until the middle of the fifteenth century that work was begun on the great tower. The nave, which had fallen into disrepair at the time of the Black Death, was finally pulled down as a last resort in 1543; it was not finally replaced until 1868, work being completed twenty years later.

Bristol Cathedral has many notable features; they include some attractive misericords, some fine vaulting, and the twin west towers that bear the names of Bishop Butler and Edward Colston. Bristol is unusual in that the nave and aisles are housed beneath the same roof, not separate roofs on different levels as in most churches.

BRECHIN CATHEDRAL
Angus

Brechin Cathedral, founded by King David I at the same time as he founded Dunblane Cathedral, in 1150, is today employed as the local parish church. It is not the first church to have stood on this site, however; for apart from the fact that tradition holds that this was the place of worship of an ancient community of Druids, a church was established here in the year 990, one of the 300 mission colleges established in Scotland at that time owing allegiance to the mother church of Iona. The famous round tower with which Brechin is today always associated dates from this era or soon afterwards, probably erected as a defensive tower and beacon combined, but having ecclesiastical associations. It is one of only three in the whole of Scotland, the other two being at Egilsay, in the Orkneys, and Abernethy.

Little is known of King David's cathedral before the fourteenth century. Unfortunately it suffered at the hands of restorers (sometimes referred to as 'vandals') several times over the centuries. Most positive among these alterations took place in the year 1806, when the transepts were removed and new aisles added; because the persons responsible for this alteration were dissatisfied with the original nave arches they had new ones constructed, raising the walls in order to allow the roof to cover the whole interior in one span, and thereby virtually obscuring the clerestory windows.

This is but one of the alterations the cathedral has suffered over the years.

Brechin Cathedral and Round Tower

Despite such disadvantages, with the exception of the fourteenth century tower and spire, it stands reasonably as originally conceived, one of the curios of Scottish episcopal activity. The ruins of the 'Maison Dieu', or hospitium, founded by William of Brechin in 1256, stand close by.

III BUILT FOR SECULAR CANONS

YORK MINSTER
Yorkshire

Sometimes called 'The King of Cathedrals', York Minster traces its architectural history back to 627, in which year Paulinus built a wooden church here. The following year this was replaced by a Saxon stone church, parts of which are to be seen to this day in the crypt. It was following the Norman conquest that work on the present structure properly got under way, under Thomas of Bayeux, who began the nave and transepts in the year 1070. These transepts were replaced in the middle of the thirteenth century and the Norman nave was rebuilt at the close of the same century and the beginning of the next. The choir and Lady Chapel date from the closing decades of the fourteenth century, and the great central tower from the early part of the fifteenth century. The north and south western towers date from the middle of the fifteenth century.

York's principal external glory is its magnificent west front. Above the entrance is a large eight light window, one of 125 windows inserted in the cathedral's walls, many of them containing the lovely medieval stained glass for which York is justly famous. The glass in the great east window and in the 'Five Sisters' window is particularly fine. By contrast much of the tracery work in the windows at York is of somewhat inferior quality.

Within, one's first impression is of the immensity of the cathedral (the largest original Gothic cathedral in England). The

York Minster

nave is both long and high (262 feet in length and 99 feet high), flanked by towering piers and a colossal vaulted roof. The north and south transepts are equally grand in their conception and in the south transept may be inspected the earliest part of the present cathedral, with some fine Early English architecture in evidence.

York is fortunate in its chapter house, one of the most lovely to be seen in this country. The choir and Lady Chapel are also quite magnificent; while throughout the cathedral there is much carving of interest and there is a fine choir screen, erected in 1500. There are many fine tombs that are well worth inspecting, the most unusual of them being that of Archbishop Walter de Grey who died in 1255 and whose coffin bears a full length port-

rait of the archbishop, its colouring extremely well preserved.

LINCOLN CATHEDRAL
Lincolnshire

Although Lincoln Cathedral is technically called Lincoln Minster it has never been the church of a monastery, having been served only by secular canons. The name however is irrelevant for this is indeed one of the major successes of English cathedral architecture, thought by John Ruskin in the nineteenth century to be the finest such building in the kingdom; and with its fine position on an eminence, completely dominating the old Roman city of Lincoln, this sentiment is not at all difficult to share.

The first cathedral in Lincoln was built by the first Norman bishop, Remigius, begun in the year 1074 and completed in 1092. There was a fire in 1141, and the third bishop restored the cathedral to an even grander condition than previously but an earthquake of 1185 destroyed much of his work and it was left to St. Hugh of Lincoln, after he had been appointed bishop, to rebuild the cathedral in the year 1192. By the time he died in 1200 he had completed the choir, the aisles and the east transept, the first manifestations of the lovely Early English style of architecture.

During the first half of the twelfth century the nave was slowly completed and the great central tower was begun. The lovely Angel Choir dates from the second half of the same century. Created to house the remains of St. Hugh, it is a fine example of the Transitional style of architecture that fell between the Early English and Decorated periods.

Lincoln Cathedral came perilously close to demolition during the time of the Civil War, when the Cromwellian soldiers wished to pull the building down. They were prevented from doing this but they never-

Lincoln Cathedral—
The West Front

Hereford Cathedral

theless succeeded in wreaking a very marked havoc, which required all the ingenuity of Bishop Fuller, who took office after the Restoration, to set right. Despite this desecration and the destruction of many important monuments and much fine glass, Lincoln remains to all outward appearances quite perfect, its graceful west front still delighting visitors to the city. Within it is equally majestic, with many fine windows and much stone and wood carving of interest. The cathedral demonstrates how century by century the great ecclesiastical establishments of Britain have encouraged the arts; most recent among its importations is a small chapel with mural paintings by Duncan Grant. In its fine library the cathedral possesses one of the four surviving copies of the Magna Carta.

HEREFORD CATHEDRAL
Herefordshire

The present cathedral at Hereford was begun in 1079 by Robert de Losinga, although the see itself dates back to much earlier times, some authorities claiming that it existed in the sixth century. Today it embodies a considerable variety of different architectural styles, having been rebuilt and added to at many different periods.

During the first half of the twelfth century, in the reign of Stephen, the cathedral suffered greatly, and for a time was deserted, its bishop being forced to flee. William de Vere, who became bishop at the end of the twelfth century, was responsible for a good deal of rebuilding, particularly at the east end of the cathedral. The Early English Lady Chapel dates from the period just after his bishopric.

The cathedral became deserted a second time during the reign of Henry III, the bishop being finally imprisoned for abandoning his see. Another period of concentrated building came during the time of Bishop Swinfield (1283-1317), who began both the eastern transept and the central tower. During the fifteenth century the cloisters and the great east window were added. During the Civil War Hereford was besieged, and the cathedral ransacked; but perhaps the greatest disaster occurred in 1786, when the great western tower collapsed, destroying with it the entire west front. James Wyatt, called in to restore the building, built a new west front, destroyed much surviving Norman work and generally transformed the cathedral.

The west end was again rebuilt at the beginning of the twentieth century.

Fortunately Hereford retains many of its finer features and is still among the most impressive of English cathedrals. It also boasts many treasures, including a library of chained books totalling some 1,500 volumes and a magnificent 'mappa-mundi' by Richard of Haldingham, dating from the late thirteenth century.

CHICHESTER CATHEDRAL
Sussex

Chichester Cathedral is of especial interest for several reasons: on account of its smallness, for its detached belfry—the only one in Great Britain—and for the unrivalled opportunity it presents to in-

Chichester Cathedral

Ripon Cathedral

spect the continuous growth and progress of medieval ecclesiastical architecture in this country, building having been carried out from the late eleventh century right up until the time of the dissolution under Henry VIII. It stands on the site of a much earlier church, that of St. Peter's monastery, first selected as his cathedral by Stigand about the year 1080, the building of the present structure being initiated by the third Norman bishop, Ralph de Luffa. It was completed in the year 1110, though four years later fire struck the building and wrought considerable havoc.

Ralph set to work rebuilding his cathedral, but it was not finally consecrated until 1148, 25 years after his death. Fire struck again in 1186, thus necessitating further rebuilding, at a time when the English Gothic style of architecture was in the process of being born. The upper storey of the western towers and the lower storey of the central tower survive from this period.

A succession of bishops supervised refinements and additions throughout the thirteenth century, during which time the nave was remodelled, chapels and porches were added and the Lady Chapel, not completed until the fourteenth century, was begun. The fifteenth century, with the ascendancy of the Perpendicular style of architecture, saw the completion of the detached bell tower and the cloisters. The central tower of the cathedral collapsed in 1861, causing much damage to the rest of the structure. It was replaced in 1866 with a replica.

Among the treasures of Chichester are the two blocks of Purbeck stone with carvings depicting the legend of Lazarus now set into the eastern piers of the crossing and reckoned to be among the masterpieces of medieval sculpture.

Ripon Cathedral—The Choir Screen

RIPON CATHEDRAL
Yorkshire

Among British cathedrals Ripon is unique for its bishopric having remained in abeyance for some 1,150 years, from 686 until 1836. The first minster here was established in about the year 657, though on a different site; in 681, on the site employed today, the church rose to cathedral status, but only for five years. It later became the church of a college of secular canons and in this capacity it was dissolved by Henry VIII when he suppressed the monasteries.

The original crypt of St. Wilfrid, dating from 661, is still preserved, but the church it served was replaced early in the twelfth century by a Norman structure. Most of this building also disappeared, making way for the present structure during the late twelfth or early thirteenth centuries, Arch-

bishop Roger of York authorising the complete destruction of the earlier building in order to begin entirely afresh, as at York.

The principal feature of this new collegiate church, which also served as a parish church, was its nave, unusual for having no aisles but this suffered at the hands of renovators during the sixteenth century and few traces remain. Other parts of the church also underwent severe alteration, although the dissolution put a halt to further building activities.

When Ripon became a bishopric for the second time its first bishop was Charles Longley, who later became Archbishop of Canterbury. In 1861 Sir Gilbert Scott was commissioned to renovate the cathedral and it is the result of his sympathetic work that may be inspected today. Among the many attractions of this cathedral are the fifteenth century choir screen and a considerable amount of fine wood carving on the choir stalls, particularly some of the misericords.

EXETER CATHEDRAL
Devonshire

The statuary adorning the west front of Exeter Cathedral immediately identifies the building, set up at the end of the fourteenth century. It consists of three rows of figures of kings, saints and warriors and was completed about 1370, more than 200 years after the present structure was first conceived by William the Conqueror's nephew, William Warelwast.

Little remains of Bishop Warelwast's building, the cathedral having suffered greatly from both local unrest and fire, so that of the original Norman structure all that can be inspected today are the two towers at the ends of the transepts, and of these the north one has undergone considerable refinement over the centuries. It was in 1258, upon the election of Walter Bronescombe to the bishopric, that serious rebuilding of the cathedral began. He and his successor were responsible for the Lady Chapel and adjoining chapels, together with the north and south transepts. The choir, nave, porches and west front followed during the early and middle decades of the fourteenth century. It was Bishop Grandisson, responsible for the final building work during the fourteenth century, who assumed such power within his see that he felt justified in refusing the Archbishop of Canterbury admission to his cathedral and even went so far as to encounter the Archbishop at the cathedral gates together with a band of armed followers.

Exeter Cathedral—The West Front

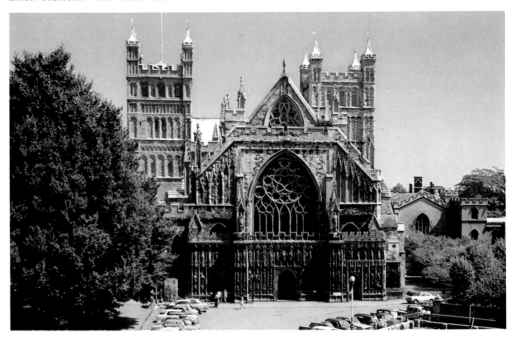

Apart from the impressive west front (where one or two of the sculptures are modern replacements) and the two Norman towers, the most notable features of Exeter Cathedral are the Gothic vaulting over the nave, dating from the fourteenth century and some 300 feet in length, a fine choir in the Decorated style, with some wonderfully carved bosses on the roof, an east window with some attractive fifteenth century glass and finally many interesting tombs and memorials.

KIRKWALL CATHEDRAL
Orkney islands

The cathedral to St. Magnus at Kirkwall, on Mainland, one of the Orkney Islands, has the distinction of having been originally under the episcopal supervision of the Archbishopric of Drontheim in Norway, the Orkneys having at one time belonged to Norway. The cathedral was founded by the Norwegian Earl Ronald, in the year 1137, and was designed by King Kol, who also supervised its construction.

Magnus was a Norwegian earl, whose father had been present at the Battle of Stamford Bridge, when King Harold, later to meet his death at Hastings, defeated King Harald of Norway and his invaders. Magnus was distinguished in the Orkneys for his embracing Christianity and for his refusal to take up arms in battle, preferring instead to face his enemies, psalter in hand. He met his death by execution, at the hand of his own cousin in the year 1115.

The cathedral which is dedicated to him is a most attractive structure, containing a fine nave of eight bays. One of the most immediately compelling features of the

Exeter Cathedral—The Nave

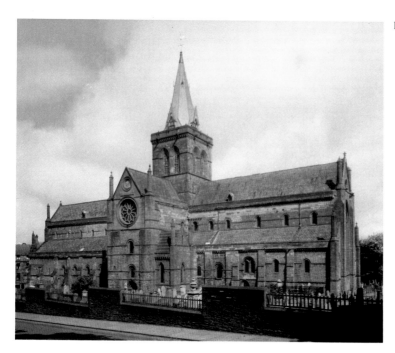

building is the fact that it is built of varicoloured stone, red and yellow sandstone blending attractively with one another. The cathedral has three west doors while the tower boasts good fifteenth century windows. Much restoration has taken place here, but the overall effect is still very pleasing.

DORNOCH CATHEDRAL
Sutherland

Dornoch was created a Royal Burgh in 1628 but its one-time cathedral church, see of the Bishops of Caithness, was built during the thirteenth century. It is claimed that the see was the foundation of King David I of Scotland, established at some date between 1146 and 1150, in all like-

lihood because there already existed a Celtic monastic house on the same site. However, it was only under the primacy of Bishop Gilbert during the first half of the thirteenth century that the see was properly constituted, and he it was who planned the building of a new church. He allowed for a chapter of ten secular canons, one of them a bishop and another the Abbot of Scone.

In 1570 the cathedral suffered considerable damage; although this was repaired, by the fourth decade of the nineteenth century it was found necessary to rebuild the nave completely and in 1924 further restoration was undertaken. Among the many interesting features of this attractive little church is a statue of the first Duke of Sutherland, who died in 1833; it is said, indeed, that sixteen of the Earls of Sutherland are buried here. In the

78

church also there is an effigy of the cathedral's founder, Bishop Gilbert.

WELLS CATHEDRAL
Somerset

The glory of Wells cathedral is its west front, a magnificent screen that has been described as a large-scale piece of stone sculpture, beautified with one of the finest arrays of medieval figure carving to be seen anywhere in Great Britain, and even though it is being partly replaced by modern work sufficient remains to remind one of its original grandeur.

Traditionally the church is said to have been founded in 704 or 705; it was accorded full cathedral rank in 909. The old church on this site was rebuilt during the middle part of the twelfth century, under the auspices of Bishop Robert but his church also was largely rebuilt during the latter decades of the same century by Bishop Reginald FitzJocelyn. However, it required until the middle of the fifteenth century for this lovely cathedral to achieve its point of perfection, when Bishop Beckington completed the cloisters.

A succession of disasters then struck the cathedral, ranging from Civil War destructiveness to nineteenth century 'restoration', but despite these misdeeds the building remains as a jewel among English churches, even though it is among the smaller cathedrals. Apart from its west front its attractions include a magnificent nave, with wholly impressive clustered columns, some exquisite stone carvings in the

Dornoch Cathedral

south and north transepts, including a man with toothache in the south transept and a woman with toothache in the north, as well as numerous other curious sculptures, a lovely choir and some fine misericords.

Without, there is also much to admire, including the 182 foot high tower, Early English in style up to roof level. There is in addition an impressive octagonal chapter house with some interesting gargoyles. The Bishop's Palace was restored during the nineteenth century, but it still represents one of the finest such thirteenth century residences in the country. Finally, there is an important library, containing numerous old books and manuscripts. Among its prize possessions is an edition of Aristotle with marginal notes in the hand writing of St. Erasmus.

LICHFIELD CATHEDRAL
Staffordshire

Lichfield Cathedral possesses many notable features: its west front, richly decorated with statuary, and its three spires, known as the 'Ladies of the Vale', which are the only grouping of three spires to survive in England. Lichfield is also worthy of attention on account of its having been one of the largest episcopal sees in early times, incorporating such later dioceses as Liverpool and Worcester, Hereford and Leicester.

The date of origin of the present structure is set at about 1190, building continuing almost without cease until about 1350. An original Norman cathedral was slowly swept away, so that no trace now remains.

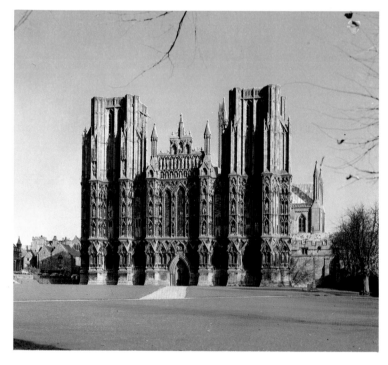

Wells Cathedral—
The West Front

80

One of the first parts of the new structure to be erected was the choir, though little of it remains today. This was followed, about 1220, by the transepts, Early English replacing Norman in architectural style. The nave followed about 1250, with the central tower and chapter house originating at the same time. The west front dates from the last decades of the same century.

In 1296 the most famous of all Lichfield's bishops was appointed to the see; this was Walter Langton, Treasurer of England during the reign of Edward I. He it was who began the lovely Lady Chapel with its octagonal apse that today contains some fine sixteenth century stained glass. This chapel was finished by Langton's successor, and with its completion the entire cathedral was finished, a fine example of Early English Gothic. It suffered a state of siege during the Civil War, causing serious desecration. Why this should have occurred may be attributed to the fact that the extremely powerful Langton had chosen to surround his cathedral with fortifications, which later allowed the Royalists actually to garrison the precincts of the cathedral. Among other tragedies, the spire was toppled by the strike of a cannon ball. It required the Restoration of the Monarchy to signal the restoration of this cathedral; though unfortunately eighteenth century 'restoration' led to considerable eclipsing of the cathedral's proper merits, mercifully righted by Sir Gilbert Scott in the nineteenth century.

The patron saint of Lichfield is St. Chad. Among the treasures of the cathedral is the St. Chad Gospel, written down and illuminated about the year 720.

Lichfield Cathedral

ST. DAVID'S CATHEDRAL
Pembrokeshire

The history of this impressive cathedral in Great Britain's smallest city is of considerable interest. St. David himself is said to have founded the see during the sixth century. William the Conqueror, soon after his arrival in Britain, visited the church and made an offering at St. David's shrine and in 1115 Bernard, the first Norman bishop, was appointed to the see by Henry I. He left the old church as it was and it was only in the latter decades of the twelfth century that a new church was begun, being completed early in the following century.

Additions and improvements were carried out over the centuries, but the first of

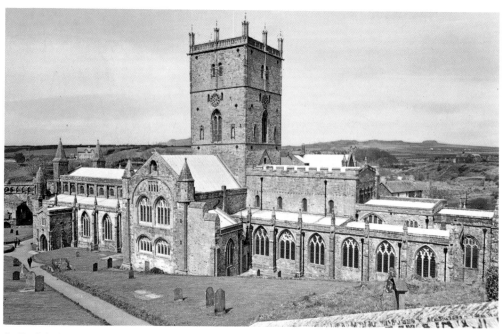

St. David's Cathedral

these was occasioned by the quite common mishap of the central tower collapsing in 1220. It was immediately replaced, but was never felt to be safe until it was attended to by Sir Gilbert Scott, who restored the cathedral in 1866. The most concentrated period of building was during the first half of the fourteenth century, under Bishop Gower; he was the person responsible for the lovely choir screen and the nearby Bishop's Palace. During the late fifteenth century much fine wood carving was introduced to St. David's and there are many intriguing misericords dating from this time. To this period also is ascribed the attractive nave ceiling, rich in decorative work.

The final touches were made to St. David's during the early decades of the sixteenth century, at which time the third stage was added to the tower. Today this is one of the principal features of the cathedral, once a major sight on the main road to the Irish ferry. The stone out of which St. David's is fashioned lends it considerable beauty, being of two colours, a local purple stone that is found nowhere else and a red stone from Dundry that dates from the fourteenth century. There is still a shrine to St. David in this cathedral, which continues to attract both visitors and pilgrims.

SALISBURY CATHEDRAL
Wiltshire

The old Norman cathedral that preceded the present building was sited within the military camp of Old Sarum. It was in the year 1220 that permission was obtained from the Pope to build a new cathedral on a more suitable piece of ground. Work began immediately and the church, with the exception of its lofty spire, was completed in the very short time of 60 years. Unlike any other medieval cathedral in England, the architect at Salisbury had the great advantage of not being called upon to incorporate any older work into his new design and could work completely afresh, producing a building some 473 feet in length, the nave alone measuring 229 feet. The upper portion of the tower, together with the 404 foot high spire, was added during the fourteenth century. The only later additions came in 1460, when supporting arches were placed in the north and south transepts and some flying buttresses were attached to the south side of the choir.

Salisbury is famous for having the tallest spire in Great Britain and for its picturesque setting, immortalised in oils by John Constable, but it has many other distinguishing features. The west front, although it has suffered from the elements in certain places and its statues have been replaced by modern works, is still extremely impressive, having five separate tiers of figures, totalling about 100. There are attractive cloisters, a lovely Early English Lady Chapel—the oldest part of the building—a library containing numerous rare books and manuscripts and an octagonal chapter house dating from the reign of Edward I.

Much of the interior decoration at Salisbury is comparatively modern, and James Wyatt caused a good deal of damage when he restored the cathedral during the eighteenth century. Among the major artistic attractions is the series of sculptures above the arcading in the chapter house, some sixty carvings in all depicting a variety of Biblical scenes.

Salisbury Cathedral

ST. ASAPH CATHEDRAL
Flintshire

The smallest cathedral to be found in England and Wales, St. Asaph can yet boast a most eventful history, having been founded during the sixth century by St. Mungo, himself driven from his northern see at Glasgow. It is claimed that there were some 965 monks and others contained within the monastery that he established here. When Mungo returned to Glasgow he left Asaph as his bishop.

The first recorded Norman bishop, in 1143, was one Gilbert, but the church which he inherited lasted only until 1283, in which year it was burnt to the ground as a result of fighting between the English and the Welsh. Work immediately began on a new cathedral, completed in 1350, but it too suffered the ignominy of military destruction, this time at the hand of Owen Glendower in 1404. Thereafter, for a period of almost 100 years, the cathedral lay in ruins.

It was in 1490 that Bishop Redman set about restoring the building and he it was who installed the east window and erected a new roof, among other improvements. His work was continued during the seventeenth century by Bishop Owen Jones, but the cathedral fell victim to the Civil War. Following this disaster not only was the Bishop's Palace transformed into a wine shop, but the cathedral itself became used for stables and cowsheds, the font being employed as a trough.

The cathedral was of course restored, but many original features disappeared for good. Certain parts of the older fabrics remain, notably some fourteenth century windows and a considerably disfigured

St. Asaph Cathedral

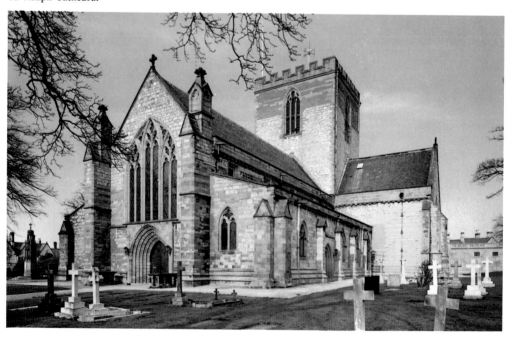

effigy of a bishop, said to be a representation of Anian, bishop at the time of the wars between Wales and England. Despite its great losses, St. Asaph remains an intriguing and attractive little cathedral.

ST. MACHAR'S CATHEDRAL
Aberdeen

Lying in the old part of Aberdeen, St. Machar's Cathedral is dedicated to its founder, a companion of St. Columba who journeyed here about the year 597. A Norman church was begun in 1183, but this was later destroyed, the present church being started in 1357 and completed during the first half of the fifteenth century. The central tower and spire, now no longer in existence, were added at a later date.

Unrest at the time of the Reformation, together with the strife of the Civil War, led to much of St. Machar's being destroyed, so that all that today remains of the little cathedral is the nave, the entire structure being only 200 feet in length. The incompleteness of the remains is more than balanced by the cathedral's unique features, including its immediately recognisable granite west front flanked by two spires dating from the sixteenth century. There is an unusual west window, consisting of seven tall, narrow openings; while within there is a fine early sixteenth century ceiling decorated with 48 heraldic shields of the princes, nobles and clerics who contributed to the cathedral's erection.

The cathedral contains much beautiful decorative work and in the charter room there is, in addition to fourteenth, fifteenth and sixteenth century charters, a collection of manuscripts, old prints and ecclesiastical records.

BEVERLEY MINSTER
Yorkshire

Beverley Minster is not of cathedral status, but the impressiveness of its architecture and its great size more than warrant its being included in these pages. The first church at Beverley was founded by St. John, late Archbishop of York, during the second decade of the eighth century. The church was added to over the years, becoming a collegiate church for secular canons during the tenth century; however, in 1188 the greater part of the structure was destroyed by fire, only the nave escaping without marked damage. The monks at once began to build the church anew, adding a central tower which promptly collapsed.

St. Machar's Cathedral

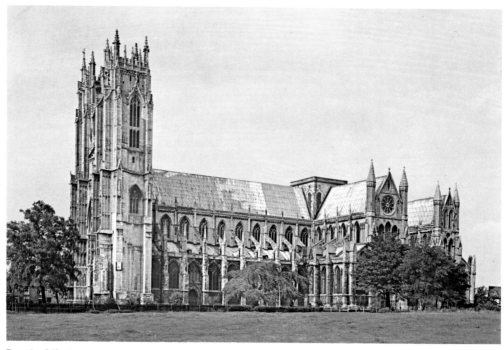

Beverley Minster

A second period of rebuilding occurred during the thirteenth century, when the monks achieved one of the finest examples of Early English architecture in the country. During the third decade of the fourteenth century the monks rebuilt the nave, completing also the magnificent west front which is today one of Beverley's glories. Thereafter building ceased, though during the eighteenth century certain decorative additions were made, fortunately destined for removal by Sir Gilbert Scott in the nineteenth century.

The only positive reminder of Beverley's Norman existence is the font but many other aspects of the present structure demand one's attention, including the fine Perpendicular west front with its twin towers and lovely window, the delicate tracery in the aisle windows and some well preserved misericords in the choir stalls. Beverley has also numerous monuments that are of considerable interest, including the tomb of the so-called 'Sisters of Beverley', probably dating from the fourteenth century but not recording either the names of the sisters or their achievements, though it is assumed that they were benefactors of the townspeople. Near the altar there is the famous Percy Tomb, erected about 1338 as a monument to Lady Eleanor Percy, richly decorated and including some fine figure sculpture.

IV POST MEDIEVAL CATHEDRALS

ST. PAUL'S CATHEDRAL
London

St. Paul's Cathedral in London, built by Sir Christopher Wren following the Great Fire, stands as an exception in these pages, being neither medieval nor modern but a fine example of the Renaissance style of architecture of which the versatile Wren was a leading exponent. The cathedral was begun in 1675 and completed in 1711, built from Wren's second design, his first having been rejected by the church authorities for not following traditional concepts of internal lay-out.

It is the dome that people think of in connection with St. Paul's, and this is in-deed its most impressive feature, having been carefully designed so that it is visible even from close up. It is surmounted by a large golden cross that stands at some 365 feet above street level. The exterior is gracefully built, and unlike earlier cathedrals its walls are not broken by large expanses of glass, Wren having deliberately kept his windows to a minimum. Within, the cathedral is rich in decorative work, boasting an ornately piered nave, a lovely choir and a superb reredos behind the High Altar.

Among St. Paul's particular features are the crypt, containing the tombs of Nelson and Wellington, together with the funeral car used to transport the latter's body to

St. Paul's Cathedral

Birmingham Cathedral—The Nave

its final resting place, the Whispering Gallery at the base of the great dome—itself consisting of an inner and outer dome —and the numerous monuments to distinguished men. Among these are the tombs of Sir Joshua Reynolds, Dr. Johnson, John Donne and Gordon of Khartoum.

BIRMINGHAM (ANGLICAN) CATHEDRAL
Warwickshire

The see of Birmingham was founded only as recently as 1905 when the parish church dedicated to St. Philip acquired full cathedral status. The church is a comparatively small one, the design of Thomas Archer and built between the years 1711 and 1719; reputedly it is a refined and much reduced version of Sir Christopher Wren's church of St. Bride in Fleet Street, London. Its most unusual feature, apart from its smallness, is its western steeple covered with a domical roof and crowned with an open lantern.

The interior of this cathedral is graced with many interesting architectural features, including arcades of square fluted piers around the arches dividing the nave from the aisles. There is also a low ironwork screen, thought to be the work of Jean Tijou, dividing the chancel from the nave. But most significant of all from the visitor's point of view are the superb stained glass windows, the design of Sir Edward Burne-Jones, presented to the cathedral by the artist towards the close of the nineteenth century, being erected between the years 1884 and 1897.

Three of these fine windows are in the east wall of the cathedral, the fourth is in the west wall. They depict the Nativity, the Crucifixion, the Ascension and the Judgment. These are among the principal features of this pleasing little baroque church, one that would not normally be taken for a cathedral. It is of interest to note that Birmingham possesses two cathedrals, the second being the cathedral of St. Chad, a Roman Catholic foundation designed by Augustus Pugin and dedicated in 1841.

Westminster Cathedral

WESTMINSTER CATHEDRAL
London

The great Roman Catholic cathedral of Westminster, almost surrounded today by towering blocks of offices and flats, was built between the years 1895 and 1910, the design of J.F. Bentley, who alas did not live to see its completion. Indeed it is still far from complete as regards its internal decoration. It was first used as a place of worship in 1903, the year following Bentley's death.

The external appearance of the cathedral is wholly unexpected, with the tall narrow tower, or campanile, known as St. Edward's Tower, set on the north side of the impressive west front. Over the west door there is a superb mosaic by R. Anning Bell, while within there is an even greater profusion of mosaic work. Within too is a lovely series of carvings of the Stations of the Cross by Eric Gill.

Westminster Cathedral, indeed, is a treasure house of works of decorative art. Its nave is the widest to be found anywhere in England, and it is punctuated by a series of pillars of white Carrara marble, all finely carved and no two of them alike. At the entrance to the sanctuary is a massive crucifix weighing some two tons, while in the Chapel of the Blessed Sacrament, situated just to the left of the High Altar, is a white marble monument erected to the cathedral's founder, Cardinal Vaughan.

Westminster Cathedral is a perfect contrast to nearby Westminster Abbey. Its attractions are of a quite different kind, but the building possesses a unique character, and a visitor to one should by no means neglect the other.

Liverpool Cathedral

LIVERPOOL (ANGLICAN) CATHEDRAL
Lancashire

Sir Gilbert Scott's massive new Anglican cathedral at Liverpool was begun in 1904, the see having been founded in 1880. The cathedral is still incomplete, though by far the greater amount of work has now been accomplished and it is possible to assess Scott's very considerable achievement.

This cathedral, the largest in Christendom with the exception of St. Peter's in Rome, embodies many interesting features. Most immediately striking of these, perhaps, is the fact that the site necessitated Scott's abandoning the traditional east-west alignment of his nave and choir. This apart, the cathedral, with a total length of 560 feet and a tower some 308

Guildford Cathedral

feet in height, follows the Gothic pattern, modified to meet twentieth century requirements. Its great size allowed for a large open central area between the two double transepts, some 200 feet in width, constituting the principal preaching area of the cathedral and allowing for very large congregations.

The cathedral contains a great deal of fine decorative work, including a magnificent High Altar; but most impressive of all is its immense size, with the height of the choir vault rising to 116 feet and that of the central area 173 feet. There is an attractive Lady Chapel, the only part of the cathedral not contributing to perfect symmetry and supported without by massive buttresses.

GUILDFORD CATHEDRAL
Surrey

Guildford Cathedral, whose foundation stone was laid in 1936, was only the fourth Anglican cathedral to be built in Britain after the Reformation. Work on the building ceased for the duration of the Second World War, and it was only in 1961 that the finished building was consecrated, in the presence of Queen Elizabeth II and members of the Royal Family. The see of Guildford was founded in 1927.

The building is the design of Sir Edward Maufe. It has simple, even austere lines, and yet its overall conception is derived wholly from the high Gothic style, adapted to fall in line with modern ideas of architecture. Its main feature is the great central tower, standing at some 156 feet; it is surmounted by a copper gilded angel 15 feet in height. The nave, which can seat up to 1,100 people, is some 365 feet in length.

Among modern church buildings in Britain, Guildford Cathedral stands high. It has many pleasing features, notably a Lady Chapel with a five-sided apse, a sculpture by Eric Gill of St. John the Baptist which stands outside the south transept, forecourts on either side of the west end of the cathedral that are enclosed by arcaded wings joining with the porch, and finally an overall impression within of both lightness and elegance.

COVENTRY CATHEDRAL
Warwickshire

The story of Coventry Cathedral is one of disaster overcome, the destruction of a fine old church by enemy bombing in 1940 and its replacement by one of the masterpieces of modern architecture, a building enriched by the addition of many contemporary artistic treasures. The old church of St. Michael, whose ruined tower and spire, together with other surviving parts, are incorporated into the overall design of the new cathedral, was raised to cathedral status only in 1918. Its story, however, stems from the fourteenth century, and even today it is possible to savour the Perpendicular grandeur of the carefully preserved ruins.

The modern structure was designed by Sir Basil Spence in 1951, the cathedral being consecrated in 1962. The design has completely broken with the medieval tradition of church architecture and apart from the preservation of a nave with flanking aisles, as well as the observance of the rule of placing the High Altar at the east end of the church, there is nothing traditional in the design.

Perhaps the most interesting feature of Coventry is its zig-zag external walling, each alternate section of the walls being pierced with windows so positioned that the sunlight plays directly on the High Altar, the remaining sections being blank. Among the treasures of contemporary craftsmanship are the world's largest tapestry, Graham Sutherland's 'Christ in Glory', placed above the High Altar, a superb baptistry window designed by John Piper and containing some 200 pieces of stained glass, and the bronze of St. Michael, by Sir Jacob Epstein, located to the right of the main porch.

92

Glossary

ABBESS—the head of a community of nuns following the Benedictine rule; sometimes employed to refer to other heads, particularly of the second Franciscan Order.

ABBEY—the habitation of a community of either monks or nuns.

ABBOT—the head of a large religious community following the Benedictine rule, and in certain instances other rules. Traditionally the abbot is looked upon as the father of a monastic family.

AISLE—an addition to the side of the nave, the latter's walls being pierced by a series of arches. Normally aisles have separate roofs, lower in height than that covering the nave and sometimes being extensions of either the chancel or transept.

ARCHBISHOP—originally a patriarch or holder of some other major see, but today the title of the head of an ecclesiastical province.

AUGUSTINIAN CANONS—the followers of St. Augustine of Hippo, originating in Italy and southern France in the middle of the eleventh century. The original followers aimed at leading lives of poverty, celibacy and obedience, imitating as they thought the ideals of the early Christians; they adopted the rule of St. Augustine, itself originating in the fifth century, after approximately half a century of existence.

BENEDICTINE RULE—the first formal monastic rule, or code of monastic conduct. St. Benedict (480-544), who wrote the rule, founded the abbey of Monte Cassino near Naples, as well as eleven other monasteries during his own lifetime. He was not however responsible for the Benedictine order as it later became constituted. The Benedictine rule formed the basis for all early Christian monastic activity, and later rules all developed from it.

BISHOP—the title bestowed upon the highest order of minister in the Christian Church. A bishop has power to confer Holy Orders and to administer the service of confirmation; he rules a diocese or a territory included within an archbishopric. His throne is situated in his own cathedral; he wears a mitre, and has for his other symbols of office a pastoral staff, pectoral cross and a ring.

BLACK FRIARS—members of the Order of Preachers founded by St. Dominic, and usually referred to as Dominicans. The name derives from the black mantle the friars wore.

BLACK MONKS—Benedictine monks who wore black habits.

CANON—a term that originally referred to all clergy on the official staff of a diocese, but which became limited eventually to secular clergy attached to a cathedral or collegiate church. Before about the eleventh century many canons owned private property and did not always live in a religious community; later those assuming this way of life were known as 'secular canons', to distinguish them from regular Augustinian canons.

CANONS REGULAR—a community of canons living under religious rule, originating in the eleventh century. During the twelfth century most of them accepted the rule of St. Augustine.

CARMELITE ORDER—the 'Order of Our Lady of Mount Carmel', founded in Palestine c.1154 by St. Berthold, though claiming descent from the ancient hermits of Mount Carmel, and even from Elijah himself. Adherents observed absolute poverty, solitude and total abstinence from flesh. Members of the order fled to Europe following the collapse of the Crusades; in England St. Simon Stock reorganised members of the order along the lines of the mendicant friars. The main objects of the order were contemplation, missionary work and the study of theology.

CATHEDRAL—a church containing a bishop's official seat, itself now usually situated on the north side of the sanctuary. In medieval Britain there were only 17 cathedrals: Canterbury, Carlisle, Durham, Ely, Norwich, Rochester, Winchester and Worcester, all cared for by monks; and Chichester, Exeter, Hereford, Lichfield, Lincoln, London, Salisbury, Wells and York, all in the possession of secular canons. After the dissolution of the monasteries Henry VIII created six new sees: Bristol, Chester, Gloucester, Oxford, Peterborough and Westminster (though the last was suppressed in 1550). In modern times the first new diocese was Ripon, created in 1836. Whereas at one time a bishop normally cared for the affairs of his own church, from the middle ages onwards a chapter was formed to see to the routine matters of administration.

CHANCEL—that part of a church located to the east of the nave and transepts; previously restricted in meaning to the area of the church in the immediate vicinity of the altar.

CHAPTER HOUSE—the building employed for meetings of a cathedral or monastic chapter, frequently erected as a separate building from about the ninth century onwards.

CHOIR—normally employed to define the part of a church where the clergy is seated.

CHURCH—from the Greek kuriakon, technically meaning something belonging to God.

CISTERCIAN ORDER—an order of white monks who took their name from the mother house at Cîteaux, founded in 1089 by St. Robert of Molesme. The Cistercians followed a brand of Benedictinism of extreme strictness. The most famous son of Cîteaux was St. Bernard of Clairvaux, who entered the establishment in 1112.

CLUNIAC ORDER—named after the monastery at Cluny, near Macon in Burgundy, founded in 910. Under the encouragement of its second abbot the high standard maintained at Cluny spread as a movement into both Italy and France. The movement's objects included the observance of strict Benedictinism, devotion to personal spirituality and concern for ceremony. The movement organised itself on a sound economic footing, eschewing lay financial control. During the eleventh and twelfth centuries the Cluniacs became exceedingly influential in the Church, although their leaders declined high ecclesiastical office. The first English Cluniac house was St. Pancras at Lewes, Sussex.

CONVENT—technically a meeting or association of men for some particular reason. In its religious connotation it refers either to a building or to those inhabiting it. Originally it applied to either sex; today it applies almost exclusively to females.

DIOCESE—the ecclesiastical territory governed by a bishop, divided into parishes. A bishop reigns with complete authority in his diocese, although in recent times the Roman Catholic bishops have had to accept increasing delegation from the Pope.

DOMINICAN ORDER—an order of friars, sometimes referred to as the Friars Preachers, devoted to preaching and study. It was the first religious order to abolish manual labour. It came into being, under the tutelage of St. Dominic, at the General Chapters of Bologna in 1220 and 1221, and spread rapidly throughout Europe. Its adherents lived in corporate poverty, owning no property other than houses and churches and living in part by begging. The rule of poverty was revoked in 1465.

FRANCISCAN ORDER—an order of Friars Minor founded by St. Francis of Assisi in 1209. His original rule has vanished, and in its present form it dates from 1223. The rule insists on complete poverty, both for individuals and for the order as a whole. Members of the order were expected to live by the work of their own hands, and if need be from begging, though they were forbidden to accept money or to own property. When the strictness of the rule was discovered to be impracticable two distinct schools developed: the 'Spirituals', who zealously followed the letter of the rule, and the remainder, who were in a majority, who relaxed it somewhat. The debate that arose from this division was finally resolved by John XXII in 1317-18, who ruled in favour of moderation.

FRIAR—a title given to a member of one of the mendicant orders, usually distinguished by the colour of their mantles. In addition to the Grey, Black and White Friars, there were also Austin Friars, Trinity (or Red) Friars and Crutched (or Crossed) Friars.

GREY FRIARS—friars of the Franciscan order, so named from the colour of their habit, subsequently changed to brown.

LADY CHAPEL—a chapel dedicated to the Blessed Virgin Mary, a part only of a larger church and usually placed to the east of the High Altar.

MENDICANT FRIARS—members of any order in which it was forbidden to own property in common. As distinguished from monks, the mendicants worked or begged for their living; they were not bound by a vow of 'stability' to any one religious establishment.

MINSTER—originally meant any monastery, monastic establishment or its church; it more frequently applies either to a church originally attached to a monastery or to a church attached to a house or college of secular canons (eg. York, Lincoln, Beverley).

MITRE—the headdress of a bishop of the western church, originally manufactured from white linen but today usually made from satin, itself frequently richly jewelled. In shape the mitre resembles a shield, and two lappets hang down the back. Other prelates than bishops have sometimes been granted the privilege of wearing the mitre, notably certain abbots.

MONASTERY—the house of a religious community. Contrary to general belief and practice, the term is not applied exclusively to male foundations.

MONASTICISM—a form of religious life intended to achieve a greater degree of perfection and stability than secular life allows. Monks vow to observe poverty, chastity and obedience, and their lives consist of work and prayer. Christian monasticism originated in Egypt under St. Antony; it was introduced in the west during the fourth century.

MONK—a term used to refer to any member of a male religious community.

NAVE—the area in a church, assigned to the congregation, that lies between the main (western) entrance and the chancel and choir. It is normally flanked by aisles.

NUN—a term used to refer to any member of a female religious community observing the vows of poverty, chastity and obedience. In Roman Catholic canon law only those who have taken 'solemn vows' are defined as nuns; the rest are sisters.

PREMONSTRATENSIAN CANONS—followers of the Order of St. Norbert (and hence called the Norbertines in England), founded at Prémontré, near Laon, in 1120. Its members followed the rule of St. Augustine, introducing additional austerities, including abstinence from meat. The order came under Cistercian influence through Norbert's friendship with St. Bernard of Clairvaux. The first English house was Newhouse in Lincoln, established c.1143.

PRIOR—the head of a priory.

PRIORESS—the head or deputy head of certain houses of nuns. In an abbey she is deputy to the abbess. Technically, in the Roman Catholic canon law, the title of prioress is confined to the head of houses that have received Papal approval and whose members have taken 'solemn vows'.

PRIORY—a religious house headed by a prior or prioress. Frequently a priory is of lower standing than an abbey. Thus under the Benedictine rule there are conventual priories (self-governing) and obedientiary priories (dependent on abbeys). In certain Roman Catholic orders, particularly the Augustinian, a priory is the customary monastic unit.

REREDOS—the decorative screen, carving, curtain or painting placed behind an altar.

SACRISTY—the annexe to a church where sacred vessels, etc. are stored; it is also used as a robing room for the clergy.

SANCTUARY—that part of the church where the altar is situated. If there is more than one altar the term is applied to the area surrounding the High Altar.

SEE—the official 'seat' or 'throne' of a bishop; now commonly employed to refer to the place in which the bishop's cathedral is located.

WHITE FRIARS—Carmelite friars, so named because of the colour of their cloaks and scapulars.

WHITE MONKS—monks of the Cistercian order, so named from the colour of their habit, manufactured from undyed wool.

Index to Illustrations

Bath Abbey	16	Lincoln Cathedral—The High Altar	70
Beverley Minster	86	Lincoln Cathedral—The West Front	71
Birmingham Cathedral—The Nave	88	Lindisfarne Priory	14
Bolton Priory	29	Liverpool Cathedral	90
Brechin Cathedral	68	Melrose Abbey	38 & 39
Bristol Cathedral	65	Neath Abbey	34
Bristol Cathedral—Norman Chapter House	66	Norwich Cathedral	59
Buckfast Abbey	17	Peterborough Cathedral—The West Front	60
Caldey Abbey	46	Pluscarden Priory	22
Canterbury Cathedral	51	Prinknash Abbey	23
Cartmel Priory	32	Prinknash Abbey—From The West	24
Castle Acre Priory	43	Rievaulx Abbey	36
Chichester Cathedral	73	Ripon Cathedral	74
Christchurch Priory	27	Ripon Cathedral—The Choir Screen	75
Coventry Cathedral	92	Rochester Cathedral	54
Dornoch Cathedral	79	Romsey Abbey	21
Dryburgh Abbey	44	St. Albans Abbey	52
Dundrennan Abbey	40	St. Albans Abbey—The Gateway	53
Dunfermline Abbey	18	St. Asaph Cathedral	84
Dunkeld Cathedral	61	St. David's Cathedral	82
Durham Cathedral	56	St. Machar's Cathedral	85
Durham Cathedral—The High Altar	57	St. Osyth Abbey—The Gateway	25
Egglestone Abbey	45	St. Paul's Cathedral	87
Ely Cathedral	55	Salisbury Cathedral	83
Exeter Cathedral—The Nave	77	Sherborne Abbey	20
Exeter Cathedral—The West Front	76	Southwark Cathedral	62
Fountains Abbey	37	Southwark Cathedral—Shakespeare Memorial	63
Furness Abbey	33	Sweetheart Abbey	42
Glasgow Cathedral	64	Tintern Abbey	35
Glastonbury Abbey	12	Waltham Abbey	26
Glastonbury Abbey—The Abbot's Kitchen	13	Waltham Abbey—The Gateway	26
Gloucester Cathedral	49	Wells Cathedral—The West Front	80
Guildford Cathedral	91	Westminster Cathedral	89
Hereford Cathedral	72	Whitby Abbey	15
Inchcolm Abbey	30	Worcester Cathedral	50
Jedburgh Abbey	31	Worksop Priory—The Gatehouse	28
Kirkstall Abbey	41	Wymondham Abbey	19
Kirkwall Cathedral	78	York Minster	69
Lichfield Cathedral	81		